CALGARY

SECRETS OF THE CITY

CALGARY

SECRETS OF THE CITY

James Martin

ARSENAL PULP PRESS

VANCOUVER

ARSENAL PULP PRESS
103-1014 Homer Street
Vancouver, B.C.
Canada V6B 2W9
www.arsenalpulp.com

Canada The publisher gratefully acknowledges the support of the
Government of Canada through the Book Publishing Industry
Development Program for its publishing activities.

Book design by Lisa Eng-Lodge
Production Assistant Judy Yeung
Photographs, unless otherwise indicated, by Zoltan Varadi
Cover photo by Blaine Kyllo
Printed and bound in Canada

Efforts have been made to locate copyright holders of source material where
possible. The publisher would appreciate hearing from any copyright holders
of material used in this book who have not been contacted.

CANADIAN CATALOGUING IN PUBLICATION DATA:
Martin, James, 1970-
    Calgary: secrets of the city

    ISBN 1-55152-076-1

    1. Calgary (Alta.)-Guidebooks. I. Title.
FC3697.18.M37 1999   917.123'38043   C99-910942-1
F1079.5.C35M37 1999

c o n t e n t s

"A new beginning for you
Treasure all of the time you spend
Calgary is your journey's end
Come now, now, now, now"
– "Neighbours of the World"
Tom Loney & Barry Bowman (1987)

"Come to Calgary, the Aquarium City. Full of sharks! Boozorium Park!
Seize your opportunity! Do not delay! Come early and avoid the future
residential district of Calgary, beautifully situated in the midst of the
unparalleled scenic beauties of the bald headed prairie, on a site
famed for its badger and gopher holes and renowned in song and story
for its entire absence of water. A pleasant place for a murder.
Rural mail service promised before the turn of the century."
– Bob Edwards
Eye Opener (October 25, 1911)

"My friend is thinking of starting a toenail museum."
– anonymous caller
Calgary: Secrets of the City hotline (1999)

Landmarks & Destinations

A W.O. Mitchell character once dubbed a certain Calgary landmark "the only six-hundred-foot concrete erection in the British Commonwealth." These pages, however, also sing the praises of less-phallic sights: mermaids, fossils, buried human hearts, garbage-eating dinosaurs, and Elvis shrines.

Photo: Kaya Wiggens

s i z e   m a t t e r s

Nobody can say for certain how closely Husky Oil was monitoring the 1962 opening of the Seattle Space Needle. Still, it's rather suspicious how the Calgary Tower (*né* Husky Tower, completed in '68) ended up edging out the Needle by a mere ten feet. Coincidence or competition? You be the judge.

s e c r e t   o b s c e n i t y

In 1967, the Universal Bolt Company in Inglewood erected an eyegrabbing rooftop sign: a giant "U" with a bolt through it. The hookers hanging around the nearby National Hotel began calling it "the Screw You sign" and – what with hookers being notorious vernacular trend-setters – the nickname stuck for almost twenty years. The sign was taken down in '94, and now rusts in peace out back.

Its frontier theme-park façade marks the newsstand/ souvenir shoppe at 131-8th Ave. SW as yet another cheesy attempt to cash in on Calgary's cowboy heritage. So who woulda thunk that it actually *is* an old west relic? In fact, it's the oldest wooden frame structure in downtown Calgary. The big fire of 1886 razed most of the city centre, but lucky #131 somehow beat the heat — quite the feat, considering buildings on both sides burnt to the ground. Pay your respects by buying a $4.99 cotton-poly "Canada" T-shirt. (The 1886 fire, by the way, is why Calgary has so many sandstone buildings: taking a cue from the three little pigs, Calgarians rebuilt the downtown with a less fire-friendly material.)

Another unassuming relic is the Hunt House, located in the backyard of the Deane House *(806-9th Ave. SE)*. Nobody can agree as to who built it or when — it's either a Hudson's Bay Co. building (1876) or a Métis buffalo hunter's shanty (1875) — but it's Calgary's oldest building still on its original site. The one-room shack is now covered with peeling blue shingles, but from inside you can see that it's an honest-to-goodness log cabin. Nobody has occupied it since W.J. Hunt vamoosed in the '60s; the building now contains unused patio furniture and a huge stack of empty booze bottles courtesy of the Deane House restaurant. (The Deane House, by the way, was built on the other side of the Elbow River in 1906 then dragged by tractor to its present site twenty-three years later.)

From a View to a Thrill

A veteran balloonist confided that he frequently gets a naked eyeful (rooftop nudies, unsuspecting highrise dwellers) while flying the friendly skies. And according to a downtown businessdude who long enjoyed a 10th floor office opposite a certain large hotel, "You'd be surprised by how many people start their day the naked way."

That said, here are four other swell views that aren't the Calgary Tower:

Memorial Dr. SE
(westbound, just before the Zoo)

Crescent Rd. NW
(anywhere)

Canada Olympic Park's 90 metre ski jump
(the highest point in the city, but it'll cost ya a few bucks to get up there)

Sunny Chinooks nudist camp
(just kidding)

Neigh-bourhood Stories

Forest Lawn was just the beginning of real estate's "untruth in advertising" policy. C'mon, honestly: Tuscany? The Hamptons? As for Hidden Valley, if the place really was hidden there'd be an awful lot of frustrated commuters crying along Shaganappi Trail. But as Donna Mae Humber reports in her two-volume *What's In A Name...Calgary?*, some of the city's flowery monikers are rooted in (gasp!) reality. A sampling:

Silver Springs: As far back as 1881, this area's been known for the underground spring which empties into the Bow River. Geologically-minded teens have long gathered in the gully between Silver Crest and Silverview Drives to admire the crystal waters and drink beer.

Jurassic Facts

Built in the 1930s, Dinny the Brontosaurus is the only remaining statue from the Calgary Zoo's original dinosaur park. Of course, anything that old simply *must* hold a few secrets. Dinny is no exception:

1) Despite what you may have gleaned from *Flintstones* reruns, there's no such thing as a brontosaurus. People back in the '30s were a little thick re: prehistoric matters, and what they called a "brontosaurus" is more like a clumsily-executed padosaurus. In other words, nothing that looked like Dinny ever walked the Earth.

2) Folklore has it that Dinny was originally coated with surplus bridge paint, launching the widespread falsehood that dinosaurs were bright green.

3) Dinny's stomach is full of junk. To save money on cement, workers padded his innards with whatever was handy. Because the stuffin' was encased in concrete, there's no way to conduct an autopsy without destroying the ten-tonne statue. Dinny is rumoured to be jammed with outhouses, lumber, and a Model T Ford.

Lion King Works Cheap

Photo: Blaine Kyllo

If you think fetching the boss' drycleaning is a drag, consider the tale of James L. Thompson. By the time the Centre St. Bridge was completed in 1916, the astronomical cost of statues prohibited any fancy decoration. Then an alderman recalled seeing a nifty lion sculpture sitting on the front porch of a NW house. Research yielded the craftsman behind the lion: James Thompson, a transplanted Scottish stone mason working as a city labourer. Since City Hall was already paying him to dig ditches, they figured they might as well take advantage of his pretty-boy stone-cutting hands. (Funny how art can suddenly become so affordable.) Working in a shack on the north bank of the Bow, Thompson based his four lions on London's Nelson Column. (The lions' perches are decorated with roses, shamrocks, thistles, maple leaves, and buffalo heads. Decode the nationalist symbolism for yourself.)

Thompson's only other bridge-work is less obvious but no less striking: you almost need to be floating downstream to admire the Indian Chief heads which adorn Banff's Bow River Bridge.

T.B. or Not T.B., That is the Question

Long considered one of the city's most prestigious neighbourhoods, Mount Royal has a contagious skeleton in its linen closet: until 1932, the plot of land bordered by Carleton and 10th Streets and Prospect and Dorchester Avenues SW was home to a tuberculosis sanitorium. Oh, the cheeky nerve of all that lower-class airborne bacteria.

Ranchlands: Whoa, this NW neighbourhood sits atop actual ranch land. (Formerly part of the mighty Burns empire, to be exact.) Who knew?

Pump Hill: Many people think the area's named for the windmill/pump combo built by Thomas Patton in 1910. (You can still see it at Patton Court SW.) Right idea, wrong pump. Pump Hill was actually named for an even earlier pump, the remains of which are barely visible in Crocus Park. (The park is to the left of the trails behind the Patton windmill.)

Heritage 911

Heritage homes are great and all, but they can be a real pain in the patootie. I mean, all that upkeep — wouldn't you rather own a non-historical parking lot or brand-new highrise apartments? (Just ask the good-hearted masterminds behind The Grandview, who dropped mucho dinero to incorporate the eightysomething-year-old Lang House into their 16-storey luxury condo tower.)

But if an "accident" happens to work in your favour, who's to complain? Legal eagles take note: I'm not accusing nobody of nuthin', but several heritage (and would-be heritage) sites have luckily — er, I mean mysteriously — burnt down in recent months. Check back in a year to see if any shiny new replacements have sprung forth.

The Buena Vista (1912-1999)
Long unoccupied, the much-admired Crescent Heights house *(102 Crescent Rd. NW)* was gutted by fire in February '99. The "official" cause of the blaze was hearty-partying squatters. With an unparalleled view of the city, the three-storey mansion drew weekly offers from interested buyers. Meanwhile the owner busied

Symbolism Galore

Sometimes a window is just a window, a roof just a roof. (Didn't Freud say that?) Not so at the Chinese Cultural Centre *(197-1st St. SW)*. The building's four pillars represent the four seasons. Nine is a lucky number in Chinese folklore, thusly the nine dragons on the restaurant's walls. And red is everywhere because it's the prosperity/happiness colour. Don't know the significance behind 30,000 roof tiles, but they were manufactured at the same factory which produced the tiles covering Beijing's Temple of Heaven. That's gotta count for something.

Fossils Fossils Everywhere

Six boulders were pulled from the Bow River to decorate each end of the Edworthy Park bridge (three per side). Put your reading glasses on and you'll see freshwater clam fossils imbedded in the rock.

More fossils are stuck in the Manitoba limestone pillars of the downtown A&B Sound *(140-8th Ave. SW)* — maybe one of the resident street-punks will point 'em out in exchange for a smoke. Ditto (re: the fossils, not the punks) for the mighty Ionic columns outside the Arts Centre's Jack Singer Concert Hall *(205-8th Ave. SE)*. Those particular fossils are best viewed on evenings when the Calgary Philharmonic Orchestra is performing. (Ouch, cheap shot. Sorry.)

I've Heard the Mermaids Decomposing

Banff's Indian Trading Post (né "The Sign of the Goat Curio Store," 101 Birch St.) is a wonderland of souvenir trinkets and taxidermy. (The stuffed beasts, according to a sign, "date back to the early 1900s, when attitudes toward wildlife were different than they were today." This is supposed to explain the sliced-in-half-lengthwise-and-glued-to-a-wall mountain goats?)

Way in the back room, hidden in a dusty glass display case, is that rarest of animals: a partially-decayed mermaid. Once a mainstay of P.T. Barnum-styled circuses, the seacritters were often referred to as "FeeJee Mermaids" – a far sight more exotic than "Monkey Torso Sewn To Trout Tail." The Trading Post offers little explanation beyond a yellowed clipping from *The Beaver* magazine (September 1942) describing a voyageur's encounter with a Lake Eerie mermaid. Penciled in the top margin are the words "This is all we know about this mamal [sic]."

Secret Heart

Father Albert Lacombe was one tough black robe, smashing transportation monopolies and surviving a musket-ball to the head – all in a day's work. When the padre finally gave up the ghost at the age of 89 in 1916, his heart was removed and placed in a jar. For years, nuns at the Father Lacombe Centre would take the jar down from the mantle and show it to visiting children and resident orphans. (It is unclear as to whether this was punishment or reward.) Perhaps realizing that some clumsy kid was gonna drop it sooner or later, the nuns eventually buried the heart behind the Lacombe Centre's main building, where it remains to this day.

himself with a 13-year-long battle with the Alberta Historic Preservation and Rebuilding Society, which vehemently opposed his extensive renovation plans. The fire damage was so great that the house had to be (ahem) demolished.

Father Lacombe Centre (1910-1999)

Built as an orphanage, and later home to a nursing school and addiction treatment centre, the Lacombe Centre (146th Ave. and Bannister Rd. SE) went up in smoke in April '99. Like the Buena Vista, those darn "squatters" were again to blame. Spooky note: the adjacent water tower was long rumoured to be haunted and, along with a large tin cross, was one of the few things to survive the flames.

50,000,000 Waste Disposal Fans Can't Be Wrong

The next time you drive off the Spy Hill Landfill weigh-in scales, hang a quick left at the Dwight Yoakam street sign (scout's honour!) and you'll behold Nick Manna's grassy knoll of earthly delights. It all started when the veteran Spy Hill Landfill utility man (and drummer) retrieved a discarded Elvis bust, added a wrought iron guitar and spray-painted tire, and voilà! a loving tri-bute to The King. (All within spittin' distance of the Calgary Correctional Centre. At the risk of getting shivved with a sharpened spoon, insert "Jailhouse Rock" joke here.)

The spray-painted tire is an obvious reference to Presley's fondness for fried peanut-butter-and-banana sandwiches, but what's with the plastic buffalo perched on his pompadour? Ah, but ours is not to wonder why. Ours is to eyeball all the weird stuff, and Elvis is just the beginning: Broken "naked lady" statuettes cluttering a park bench! A lawn jockey playing an unplugged electric piano! A lobotomized plaster duck frolicking in a cracked birdbath! Busted-up hobby horses surrounding a scare-crow! And more plaster gnomes than would be normally considered healthy.

Finally, a sober note. The Elvis bust you see today replaces the original, tragically smashed by heartless thugs. And so a polite request: please leave the dump exactly as you found it.

You Are So City Beautiful, to Me

The antithesis of the grid system, the "City Beautiful" design movement favoured curvy streets. In 1914, Thomas Mawson envisioned a City Beautiful look for Calgary's civic centre, and he whipped up a set of watercolour paintings to illustrate the idea. One need only stand at City Hall and look west down 8th Ave. to know his vision never came to fruition — except for Mount Royal, which is a City Beautiful oasis in a railroad grid desert. (Full disclosure: Mount Royal's curvaceous good looks are partially due to the numerous creeks which once cut through the neighbourhood, making non-linear streets a necessity. That's also why many of the homes are set so far from the street. Well, that and snobbery.) As for Thomas Mawson's watercolours, they were recently found insulating the walls of a downtown garage.

Lorraine Apartments (1914-1998)

The Lorraine (620-12th Ave. SW) was renowned for cheap rents and prime downtown location — until a January '98 fire, that is. Thirty-six tenants were left homeless. "Official" cause: an unattended burning cigarette. The building's shell is still standing, but extensive fire/water damage means a date with the wrecking ball is imminent.

A Barren Wasteland by Any Other Name

Yeah, it's got some problems, but Forest Lawn is one of the city's most interesting neighbourhoods. (You haven't witnessed "mosaic" theory in action until you've seen a Vietnamese strip mall happily coexist with the Newfoundland Store.) Maybe the root of the Lawn's bad rep is its incongruous name. During the real estate boom of 1910, a pair of American hucksters started selling bone-dry prairie land as a lush, green urban getaway: Forest Lawn. You'd think people would've balked at a town named after an L.A. cemetery, but they lined up to buy property sight unseen. The snake-oil salesmen even threw down a few old railway ties to give the impression a Calgary-Forest Lawn commuter train was being built. (The town of Forest Lawn has long since been annexed by Calgary, but they're still waiting for that damn train.) Judging the locals sufficiently fleeced, the con-men took their money and amscrayed.

Bauhaus is in the House

Strange but true: Walter Gropius, head honcho of the Bauhaus design school, was a huge fan of Canadian grain elevators. He discovered the buildings while exiled from Germany, and his enthusiasm spread to fellow design-freak Le Corbusier. Together, the two gents poured over grain-handling promotional packages, enthusing about the slip-cast concrete technology and clean functionalism. Le Corbusier even went so far as to include Calgary's federal grain elevator (now called the Alberta Terminals, and easily viewed from Deerfoot Tr.) alongside the Parthenon in his seminal *Vers Une Architecture* (1923).

Million Dollar Homesteads

A boon to busybodies, the city's "fairshare" website (www2.gov.calgary.ab.ca/fairshare) is a high-tech answer to an age-old question: "How much do you think that place is worth?" Type in any Calgary residential address and the computer will spit out the house's price-tag - as calculated for tax purposes and independent of real estate market forces. (That is, you could conceivably sell your house for twice the taxman's assessment. Or half.) All we need now is a website to answer "He doesn't work and she's a temp, so how can *they* afford a new car ?"

Avenue magazine caused a ruckus when it used the fairshare website to research "Calgary's 10 Most Expensive Homes" for its May '99 issue. It seems a lot of people felt such info was an invasion of privacy, and I couldn't agree more. I had nothing to do with said debacle, but feel an apology is in order all the same. So, on behalf of cyberspaced nosy parkers everywhere, a big wet "sorry" to the following homeowners:

The Iceman Renovateth

Local folklore has it that a wealthy contractor built himself a three-storey mansion during the 1930s. His wife, however, thought the house was far too big; she refused to move in. (All that dusting – who can blame her?) Undaunted, the contractor hit upon a genius solution: lose the second floor. The third floor was jacked-up, the second floor demolished, and #3 (now the new #2) was slowly lowered. Good idea, except the jacks stopped 12 inches shy of the desired destination. A new plan: giant blocks of ice were slipped between the floors, keeping everything in place while the jacks were removed. As the ice slowly melted, the top floor gently descended into place. Bingo! A two-storey house that even the pickiest housewife would love. Check out the icy handiwork for yourself at 222-Scarboro Ave. SW.

(Urban legend, you say? The flying goat-man down the street swears its true. Then again, he microwaves poodles.)

Mayo & Mustard on that Stunted Development?

Although brilliantly disguised with browny-yellow stucco, the three giant pillars in the alley behind the 4th St. fast-food/liquor complex (396-11th Ave. SW) are remnants of a never-realized highrise. (Telltale rebar can be seen sticking out the top.) Calgary may have lost a skyscraper, but it gained a 24-hour Robin's Donuts. And Lord knows we can never have enough Subways.

Westhills Rock City

Now home to outlet stores and obscenely huge houses, the Westhills/Signal Hill area was once a giant tent city where 15,000 fresh-faced Canadian Expeditionary Force recruits trained for the Great War. Following British tradition, the young soldiers used some 30,000 fieldstones to "write" their regimental numbers on the hillside, commemorating the 51st Canadian Infantry Battalion (Edmonton), the 137th Infantry Battalion (Calgary), the 113th Lethbridge Highlanders Infantry Battalion, and the 151st Central Alberta Battalion. Long since faded and overgrown with grass, the white-washed rocks were restored in the late '80s. The "113" rocks sit exactly where they were first laid out in 1916; the other numbers were shifted slightly east of their original location.

Double Your Pleasure, Double Your New York-Style Loft Livin' Fun

The Lewis Loft (2nd St. and 11th Ave. SW) is literally twice the building is used to be. Formerly the home of Lewis Stationery (and Ashdown's Warehouse before that), the building was originally half its present size. Not long after complettition, the builders realized they should've made the place bigger. And so they did. The seam dividing the original building from its 1912 addition runs from sidewalk to roof, and can be seen just to the right of the front doors. (The suture is even more noticeable from the back alley.) This explains the oddly asymmetrical placement of the rooftop flagpole, which would have sat smack in the middle of the original building.

Secret HQS

It's easy to figure out what's up with certain buildings, like the giant-donut-and-submarine-sandwich complex up 17th Ave. near Westbrook Mall. (It's a car dealership. Kidding!) That's why it's darn suspicious when a building has nary a sign indicating its contents. Now, thanks to state-of-the-art surveillance technology (and loose-lipped employees milling around outside on smoke breaks), I'm pleased to deliver the skinny on the following mysterious buildings:

301-11th Ave. SW
The "24 Hour Video Surveillance" signs hint at something dastardly, but it's just the CIBC cheque-processing plant.

1313-10th Ave. SW
Another cheque-processing outfit, this time belonging to Royal Bank.

1216-10th Ave. SW
Yet another of the aforementioned banking behemoths. This one is so new that the guy smoking near the front doors didn't even know which bank, and he works there.

510-12th Ave. SW
Doesn't look like much from the outside, but Suite 300 is home to the Calgary branch of the Canadian Security Intelligence Service. CSIS are notoriously tightlipped as to what they actually do, but maybe *you* can bring them out of their shell: 292-5255.

Before moving to its current sprawling industrial park digs, the *Calgary Herald* occupied a majestic building on the corner of 1st St. and 7th Ave. SW. The building's exterior was adorned with over 600 gargoyles, many of which were caricatures of *Herald* staff: stenographers, typesetters, pressmen, editors, and even the cleaning lady. The gargoyles were crafted in 1911 and '12 by Mark Villars Marshall of England's Royal Doulton, and carefully removed before the wrecking ball's strike in 1973. The city bought the bulk of the statues, storing them for 20 years before auctioning 'em off in 1994.

In addition to the gargoyles now in the hands (or living rooms, or gardens) of individual collectors, look for relocated *Herald* gargoyles outside places such as: the 7th Ave. Telus tower, the University of Calgary's Science "B" building (near MacEwan Hall), the Bata Out There store *(804 1st St. SW, formerly the*

ghost stories

As Roky Erickson once sang, "If you've got ghosts, you've got everything." If that's the case, Calgary's got it all. (Several of the following tales can be found in Barbara Smith's two volumes of *Alberta Ghost Stories*.)

take that, you little tramp

The Congress apartments *(725-13th Ave. SW)* were originally occupied by elderly rich folk no longer spry enough for their Mount Royal mansions. 'Tis rather proper, then, that the building is haunted by a snappily attired older woman. Well-dressed she may be, but well-mannered she ain't. The mischievous spirit likes to fiddle with the furnace, turn stoves on/off, and once smashed a china Charlie Chaplin figurine into smithereens.

our spooky heritage

Heritage Park Historical Village *(1900 Heritage Dr. SW)* is not only home to a great collection of old houses, but it has ghosts up the proverbial wazoo. For starters, the Prince House (once home to lumber magnate John Prince) hosts a mysterious Woman In White and her equally mysterious Infant In White. The home's third floor, sealed from human access and without electricity, is also known to light up like Christmas during the wee hours.

Sam Livingston(e), a gold prospector and so-called "first Calgarian," is said to haunt his former homestead. Nobody can agree on how to spell his surname, which may be why his spirit is so restless.

Even the Sandstone House is haunted, and it's not even a real house. The Sandstone was cobbled together using materials from three other historical buildings (ergo no one ever actually lived there), but visitors report seeing a phantom woman changing a phantom baby's phantom diaper. The ghosts' "real" identities, as well as why a phantom diaper would need changing in the first place, are unknown.

is there a doctor in the haunted house?

Nobody knows the back-story behind the shadowy presence who haunts the Coste House *(2208 Amherst St. SW)*, but everyone knows his name: Dr. Carmichael. One theory is he's the ghost of one of the wealthy Coste family's servant, left behind when they moved out of the mansion. (Sure, the Costes founded Canadian Western Natural Gas – but a *doctor* for a butler? Man, the rich really are different from the rest of us.)

deane scream

Unplugged antique phones ring. Glass cabinets shatter. Phantom figures strut about, offering unsolicited advice along the lines of "get out now." With numerous suicides, a murdered prostitute, a fatal tumble down the main staircase, gunplay on the front porch, and even death by natural causes, is it any wonder the Deane House is haunted? That said, the Deane House *(806-9th Ave. SE)* is a delightful place for afternoon tea or a Friday evening murder mystery dinner. Call 269-7747 for reservations.

back(draft) from the grave

Firefighter N. Cocks was killed during a routine drill at the #1 Firehall *(138-6th Ave. SE)* and he's still lurking around even though the building is now a Budget Rent-A-Car. Over at the Hose & Hydrant Neighbourhood Pub *(1030-9th Ave. SE, formerly Firehall No. 3)*, the staff share their tips with a monkey believed to have been torn to shreds by jealous Dalmatians.

Alberta Hotel), and perched inside the Glenbow museum (near the admission desk). According to City Hall records, only 381 of the 600 gargoyles are accounted for – meaning 219 of the stoneware critters have gone mysteriously AWOL.

Eccentric Homes & Gardens

Aren't people happy with a few plaster gnomes anymore?

21st Ave. and 18A St. SW
Wow, an honest-to-goodness geodesic dome! Buckminster Fuller would be proud.

716 Bridge Cres. NE
Residents have a great view of the Calgary Tower. The miniature Calgary Tower in their front yard, that is.

912-5th Ave. SW
For years, this house had a mini airplane half-concealed under a tarp in the front yard. Now it has the same airplane balanced on an upright post. Viva progress!

407-34th Ave. SW
A house that looks like it was built from old grain silos, and a year-round teepee in the yard – who could ask for anything more?

i love a ghost in uniform

The Lougheed House (707-13th Ave. SW) has had a lot of incarnations over the years – a World War I nurse training school, WAC barracks during World War II, home to the Red Cross – any of which could "explain" the appearance of a female ghost wearing a white gown.

free admission with proof of afterlife

As if the Stampede midway isn't crowded enough, now we gotta contend with astral plane traffic. Founding father Guy Weadick died in 1952, but is said to still roam the grounds. The mini-donuts are that good.

sit, cujo, sit (good demon-dog)

Occupants of 823-6th Avenue SW have felt the hot, sticky breath of an invisible canine huffing down their necks. Gross footnote: this supernatural experience comes complete with that patented doggie smell.

supernatural skinflints

In 1967, a cabbie reported driving A.E. Cross' ghost (dressed entirely in black) from the York Hotel to the Cross House. The ghost stiffed the driver on the $1.50 fare and disappeared into the night. Perhaps he was worried about catching hell with the missus; his wife also haunts their former home (1240-8th Ave. SE).

Another local ghost used his special status to skirt around admission fees. Decked out in WWI garb, "Sam" used to haunt the theatre at the Science Centre back when it was the Planetarium (701-11th St. SW). Because the building sits on the site of an old fort, some think Sam is the ghost of a deceased soldier with unfinished earthly business and a strong craving for Laser Zeppelin light shows.

beer: not just for the living anymore

Some pub staff believe the Rose & Crown's attic-cum-storeroom (1503-4th St. SW) to be haunted, but maybe it's just an excuse to not fetch supplies. Then again, the place used to be a funeral home so it would be weird if it *wasn't* haunted. The Rose & Crown: come for the Guinness, stay for the spectral energy disturbances.

eternal detention

The late Ernest "Stevie" Stevenson lived on the third floor of Hillhurst Community School (1418-7th Ave. NW), where he worked as a custodian. Some say he's still there, swinging doors, moving things around, and occasionally removing his portrait from the wall.

room with a ghoul

Sam McCauley hasn't let death stop him from helping guests at the Banff Springs Hotel. The deceased porter still carries luggage, shines lights into windows, and protects his hidden cache of tips. Other Banff Springs ghosts: the headless bagpiper, the bride who tumbled down a staircase and broke her neck, and the bartender who cuts off soused patrons.

breath! push! scream in terror!

Maudine Riley died while giving birth at home. Years later, her house was demolished to make way for the Grace Hospital (now the Health Resource Centre). According to hospital superstition, one particular delivery room was notorious for difficult labours – it was later determined to sit directly overtop the room in which Riley passed away.

Atypical Green Spaces

Calgary is truly blessed with a multitude of parks, from the massive (Nose Hill, Fish Creek) to the seemingly-infinite neighbourhood "tot lots." What follows are four unusual nature spots found within city limits.

Babbling Brook Park

A man-made stream runs through it – through Canyon Meadows, that is. One kilometre of re-circulated watery goodness, the way Mother Nature would've wanted it.

Burns Memorial Rock Garden

Located in the northern part of Riley Park, the garden is a bonanza of the everday (perennials, annuals) and the uncommon (snakeroot, horse chestnut). *8th Ave. and 12th St. NW*

Inglewood Bird Sanctuary

A fascinating microcosm of foothills life that would make Tippi Hedren soil her drawers. (That's a *The Birds* joke. Because it's a bird sanctuary. Get it? Sorry.) Tours available. *2425-9th Ave. SE*

weird museums

A.V. Roe Canada Heritage Museum

Located in the back of a hobby shop, the A.V. Roe Museum is dedicated to: (a) spreading the good word about the ill-fated airplane manufacturer, and (b) building a two-third scale piloted replica of the CF-105 Avro Arrow. The museum has an extensive collection of purloined blueprints. (Everything was *supposedly* destroyed when the Arrow project was ixnayed back in '59.) The staff are enthusiastic about their work and eager to chat, but be warned: brace yourself for an earful about Diefenbaker. *6802 Ogden Rd. SE, 236-5098*

Chinook Keyboard Centre

The old police station now houses a truly amazing collection of organs (pipe and electric), pianos, synthesizers, etc. Highlights include: interactive Hammond B-3s ("interactive" meaning you can tickle the ol' ivories), and Napoleon's second wife's first piano. Or maybe it was Napoleon's first wife's second piano. Either way, it's neat. *134-11th Ave. SE, 261-7790*

Movie Poster Shop

Part of this non-descript NE warehouse houses a display/maze of movie posters, ranging from classic Saul Bass to classic blaxploitation (and everything in between). That's the "museum" part. The rest of the building is devoted to posters for sale. Browsing the "sale" stacks is forbidden; would-be buyers are instead directed to the alphabetical listings of available items. (The museum/shop does boffo international business, and the inventory is dwindling accordingly. We're talking vintage posters and lobbycards rescued from theatres, not reprints – once this stuff is gone, it's *gone*.) One of the grumpy staffers will retrieve your selections for you. A musty, weird place. *9, 3600-21st St. NE, 250-7588*

Calgary Police Service Interpretive Centre

The CPSIC is a peculiar mix of titillating entertainment and scared-straight education. Entertainment highlights: a tab of "Superman" acid, snapshots of 1960s undercover cops in "hippie" garb, and the rogues gallery of guys getting arrested. (I bet the fat biker in the "We're not having fun until you're calling 911" T-shirt feels pretty stupid right about now.) Education highlights: counterfeit money, interactive police sketch terminal (draw your parents!), and a bullet removed from a murdered officer. The "Civic Pride" Award goes to a display boasting about the good street rep earned by Calgary-grown hydroponic weed. Finally, where else can you learn the three types of pimps? (For the record: "Popcorn," "Live," and "Mac Daddy.") I mean, other than the streets. *316-7th Ave. SE (upstairs), 268-4566*

Natural History Museum & Fossil Shop (Banff)

Easy to miss, but absolutely worth your while. The dusty exhibits oscillate between the legitimately impressive (fossils) and the plain weird (a piece of the Berlin Wall, "donated by Les"); all are marked with hand-scrawled descriptions jotted on bits of loose-leaf. Highlights include: milk cartons full of dinosaur vertebrae half-hidden under bedsheets, a graphically-illustrated Richter scale wall chart ("7.0-7.5: General panic"), a Hawaiian "cowdung bomb," and pictures of local animals which were clearly, shamelessly torn from books. Even better is the ratty model of Bigfoot, "based on information gathered from the over 500 reports and eyewitness accounts of Indians, prospectors, woodsmen, scientists, housewives, police officers, anthropologists, etc." *112 Banff Ave., 762-4747*

Western Heritage Centre

Dedicated to all things livestock and/or rodeo. Can't-miss-highlight: sticking your hand up a plexiglass cow's birth canal. (The jury is still out as to whether the aforementioned experience is "educational" or "scarring.") *North of Cochrane on Highway 22, 932-3514*

GARAGELAND

Magnificent sandstone buildings are a dime a dozen (Calgary prides itself on being the "Sandstone City" after all), but a sandstone *garage*?!? Take a stroll through certain Erlton alleys and you'll come across just that. The corresponding houses aren't sandstone (heck, nothing else in Erlton is sandstone), which raises the question: huh? Did turn-of-the-century homeowners "borrow" a few blocks o' rock from the nearby quarry? Or did the sandstone conveniently "fall off" the proverbial passing truck? Only one thing's for certain: would-be Sherlocks are advised to shake a leg 'cuz the evidence is disappearing fast. Damn you, gentrification.

Secret Ruins

Ruins (that is, the crumbling remains of buildings) serve as a poignant reminder of humankind's fleeting achievements, a humbling monument to time's fickle finger. Either that or they're just a great place to snap wedding photos.

All you brides and grooms can access the ruins known as "Lindsay's Folly" (a.k.a. "Deadman's Castle") by either walking down the bike path from Princess Obolensky Park (in Rideau) or up from the Elbow River. Either way, you'll see the partial remains (basically fragments of the East, North, and South walls) of a never-completed sandstone mansion dug into the side of the hill. After striking it rich with Yukon gold, Dr. Neville Lindsay began constructing his dream home in 1913. The sandstone was salvaged from the demolished Knox Presbyterian Church, and the good doc sunk $200,000 into the project before calling it quits. Generations of kids played (and still play) in the abandoned ruins, so there's the expected plethora of stories surrounding the ill-fated home. Most of the mythology involves the untimely demise of Lindsay's wife – one story has it that the heartbroken widower couldn't bring himself to finish their house, another claims he killed her after performing a botched abortion – but the boring fact of the matter is Mrs. Lindsay outlived her hubby. The history books are spotty, but the house was likely scuttled after WWI-induced money woes. Over the years, the Folly's glory was stripped away: fancy statues were unceremoniously dumped in a Queen's Park Cemetery gardener's hut, steel support beams were recycled during the war effort, and the subterranean ducts (long a fave with local tykes) were sealed in the '70s. (In the 1930s, kids chased a flasher named "Carrots" into the ducts, trapping him until policed arrived. Historians are divided as to whether his nickname was complimentary or derogatory.) Neville Lindsay's other legacy is far more distinguished: Lindsay Park.

More Kodak moments can be had at the "Rundle Ruins" (6th St. and 12th Ave. SE), which are the remains of the Calgary General Hospital. Strictly speaking, it's the remains of the General's *second* location. Completed in 1895, General #2 held 35 beds, an operating room, and a nursing school. Maternity wings followed in

Plus-15 Tour

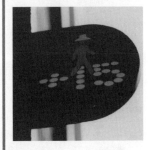

The Plus-15 system is the office drone's winter dream, allowing for quick building-to-building travel without stepping outside. With over 12 kms of climate-controlled comfort linking much of the city centre, there's no need to struggle with boots and mittens just to run that laser-copy errand.

The system was first conceived in the '60s. Since that time, a whole Plus-15 culture has developed. Take a stroll through the second-storey world during a weekday lunch-hour and you'll find all sorts of food courts, mom 'n' pop coffee spots, dry-cleaners, photocopy shops, shoe-shine stands, etc. It's like a really big airport which keeps strict reverse-vampire hours; things get to an early start in Plus-15 World, but it's basically a ghost-town after 4:30 p.m. (As for shoe-shines, only a sucker pays more than three bucks.)

French egghead Michel Tournier based his 1975 novel, *Gemeni*, on his own cross-Canada journey. The book is less than enthusiastic about Calgary's downtown: "A scorching, dust-laden wind blows through the streets, which are numbered and laid out on a grid system. The center of this concrete desert is the thirty-six-story International Hotel building, looming over a landscape as flat as your hand. . . . Skyscrapers are a natural reaction to too much space, of the terror of being surrounded by wide-open spaces, like chasms in a horizontal plane."

"Concrete desert?" *Au contraire,* Mikey. Give yourself over to the Plus-15, and you'll find yourself privy to a world o' wonders. Highlights include:

• 1946 Norseman Mark V ski-plane, suspended from the ceiling. *Petro-Canada building.*

• The skeleton of a wood bison, encased in layers of cracked glass. Two different plaques tell the story of how the mighty beast died 4,600 years ago. The skeleton was discovered in 1973, on the banks of the Glenmore Reservoir, but the plaques can't agree by whom. Was it

1899 and 1905, and a second-storey in 1903. When General #3 opened in 1910, #2 began a 44-year stint as an isolation hospital. (General #3 opened its own isolation ward in 1954, and the patients were carefully transferred in what came to be called "Operation Measles.") Before they became ruins in 1973, the Rundle building served as an United Church seniors home. Thanks to new innovations in implosion technology, the third General Hospital was reduced to dust in 1999. No ruins to speak of, but it's sure a nice gravel pit.

Secret Collection

Hidden behind the giant ant farm in the Calgary Zoo's Karsten Discovery Centre is the Biofacts Lab, a tiny room jam-packed with animal parts. (Not quite as gory as it sounds. But close.) It's basically a warehouse of artifacts that are occasionally hauled out for educational purposes, but aren't generally displayed. Some of the items are from the private collection of the Zoo's first curator (Tom Baines, the man who may have single-handedly imported black squirrels to Calgary) and others are picked up by staff during their various travels. Highlights include: skulls (pelicans, elephants, and bears – oh my!), owl talons, shark teeth, and dung beetle dung. The less "correct" items (e.g., the cookie jar made from a rhinoceros foot) are used to teach kids the importance of, well, not killing animals to make cookie jars.

Secret Tunnels

University of Calgary

Everyone's heard the legend about the underground pedestrian tunnels linking all the University's buildings, now closed due to rapes and murders. Some former students claim firsthand knowledge of the tunnels. Others mistake the mythical tunnels for the ones linking the rez buildings. Others still (who *are* all these people?) claim the steam/hot-water tunnels were once open for student traffic, now off-limits because of the obvious safety hazard. (People and super-hot pipes are a bad combo.)

There's either a whole lotta lyin' – or a whole lotta spin control – going on, but one thing's for sure: the campus is a rabbit warren of steam-pipe tunnels. Above-ground evidence can be seen next to the Phys. Ed. building's archway, where snow is extra quick to melt away from a small patch of grass. While mere mortals wander the sidewalks, workers bicycle through the mercilessly hot tunnels, checking pipe performance as they go. The occasional splash of tunnel graffiti is the only sign of the student (more precisely: the *engineering* student) body: "HRC," which stands for "Hell Raising Committee."

SAIT

More steam-pipes. Like the U of C tunnels, they ain't much to look at but they're everywhere. The ones leading into the Alberta College of Art and Design buildings have been used to host the occasional art exhibit.

Palliser Hotel

The tunnel starts in the boiler room, briefly jogs south to get underneath the train tracks, and then runs straight east. Little used today, the tunnel's purposes were two-fold: (1) to help porters sneak luggage from the train-station into the hotel, and (2) to do laundry. That's right, laundry. You'd think a ritzy joint like the Palliser would've had its own laundry, but back in the day, all the linen was cleaned at the electrical substation on the corner of 9th Ave. and 1st St. SE. (Weird, but true.) The underground laundry express has been long discontinued, but the tunnel still runs the two-block stretch to the substation.

three elementary school kids? Or a doctor and his son? So many mysteries, so little time. *Sun Life Plaza, between the escalators.*

• Lunchbox Theatre. For 25 years, the theatre has staged 50-minute plays designed to break the noontime monotony. An unexpectedly cool concept rising from deep in the heart of corporate Calgary. *Bow Valley Square.*

• Neato collection of antique gas station pumps. *Shell building.*

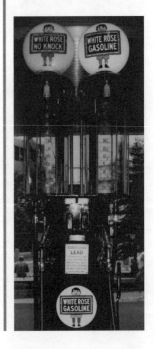

- Statue of a polar bear grimacing in pain. *First Alberta Place, lobby.*

- Secret rooftop picnic oasis in the Plus-15 intersection between Altius Centre and Caesar's Steak House. Benches, petunias, and the occasional discarded bottle of Old Milwaukee. *4th Ave. SW, between 4th and 5th Streets.*

Photo: Sven Schwirm

- Large stone globe, covered with hundreds of tiny Canada geese. The geese are stuck into the globe with pins, à la butterfly collections. What's more, the whole thing is located at the base of a waterfall. *Amoco building, lobby.*

- Actual *razor-wire* wrapped around the open-air Plus-15 which links Western Corporate Centre with the park across the street. (Y'know, the park with that statue of the guy playing chess.) Razor-wire: when barbed-wire simply won't do the trick. *8th Ave. SW, between 7th and 8th Streets.*

Mmmmmm...Beer Water

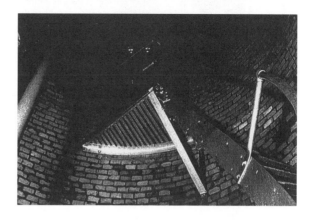

Back in its heyday, the old 9th Ave. SE brewery was quite the attraction. As a general rule, any place that makes beer is just fine with folks, but the brewery boasted additional bells 'n' whistles such as elaborate gardens, an aquarium, and tours of the inn-house well. The aquarium was short-lived (and, by many accounts, leaky) and the gardens are still nice but only a shadow of their former magnificence. The well, however, is still really cool. (Sorry, no more tours.) When A.E. Cross was first planning Calgary Brewing and Malting back in the 1890s, he'd hoped to draw his water from the Bow – until the discovery of an alluvial gravel aquifer running through his property. A 21-foot open brick well was dug, and the aquifer proved the perfect water source of CB&M's beer. (The facility's subsequent owners, O'Keefe and Molson, also brewed with aquifer water. The brewery has been dormant since '94, and it's up for sale if you're interested.) So good was the H_2O that Cross initiated the motto "It's the water!" Today, the well could use a good pool-skimming (proposed new motto: "It's the floating ball-cap!") but the water is fine as ever.

The Plus-15 above, secret tunnels below. Somewhere in-between, futuristic RocketMen buzz the Stampede Grounds while observers plug their ears in pain. All that, plus: traffic-fighting tips, tank school, and the voice of the C-Train.

In the Navy (Museum)

Given Calgary's landlocked locale, you'd be forgiven for thinking the Naval Museum of Alberta (*1820-24th St. SW, 242-0002*) has something to do with bellydancing. Until the mid-'80s, SAIT students practiced their mechanical chops on donated marine fighter planes: a Supermarine Seafire Mk. XC, a Hawker Sea Fury, and a McDonnell Banshee F2H-3. When the school no longer needed the aircraft, the three planes were returned to the Naval Reserve. As everyone and their dog knows, there's no better excuse for a naval museum than to house some vintage fighter jets. And that's why Calgary is home to the largest naval museum this side of Halifax.

Well, not quite. Truth be told, there's a tad more to the story. The Naval Museum of Alberta was also built to honour the memory of Lt. Robert "Hammy" Hampton Gray, a graduate of the Calgary Naval Reserve who has the dubious honour of being the last Canadian killed during WWII. The Royal Canadian Navy's only recipient of the Victoria Cross, Hampton fell victim to a Japanese destroyer a mere three hours before the bombing of Nagasaki.

secret plus-15

There are more than twelve kilometres of Plus-15s linking downtown buildings, but only *one* of them is south of 9th Ave. The little-known passage's rickety design (think: tin trailer perched on train trestle) and incongruous title ("Sky Walk"?) hint that it's about as official as a $20 "Rolix" wristwatch. Unauthorized hanger-on or not, the Sky Walk offers brave pedestrians a rare bird's eye view of the graffiti-covered train-tracks behind the Palliser Hotel. It also leads to a filthy stairwell which exits, of all places, onto the Bottlescrew Bill's patio.

Photo: Sven Schwinn

secret swamp road

Back in the good ol' days, a movie cost a nickel and much of Hillhurst-Sunnyside was a swampy slough. Which brings us to Gladstone Rd. NW, the 45-degree anomaly bisecting Hillhurst's otherwise orderly street-grid. The road marks the edge of what was once a particularly large bog, and serves as a poignant reminder of how far our stinkwater-pumping technologies have progressed.

Traffic!

Calgary is blessed with four waves of toe-tapping, sailor-swearing traffic:

First Wave *(5:30 to 6:30 a.m.)*
For diehard early birds only. Not a heavy flow, with mostly single-light stops.

Second Wave *(6:30-8 a.m.)*
Here's where things get sticky. The Second Wave traffic tsunami begins in the suburbs and moves inward, engulfing First Wave stragglers as it powers its way into the downtown core. Be afraid, be very afraid.

Third Wave *(around 8:30 a.m.)*
More like a wave pool variety, Wave Three consists of people who have already been to the office (First Wave keeners, no doubt) and are now making their way to 9 a.m. appointments. It's sick, really.

Fourth Wave *(begins at 4:30 p.m. and last 'til who-knows-when)*
The morning rush-hour may be spread out over a three-hour period, but not so the afternoon. With the enthusiasm of Fred Flintstone sliding down that dinosaur, tired drones evacuate the downtown salt-mines *en masse*. There's nothing you can do about it, so bring a book.

I Just Flew in from the 14th Century, and Boy Are My Arms Tired

Leonardo da Vinci, renowned for having too much time to kill, was obsessed with building an ornithopter (a.k.a. "flapping flying machine"). To this day, the ornithopter remains one of the great aviation mysteries: birds do it, bees do it, so why the hell can't *we* do it? The lobby of the Air Canada offices (*100, 333-5th Ave. SW*) boasts a non-operational, full-sized ornithopter. I think it's some sort of "triumph of the human spirit" statement. Either that, or someone from WestJet accidentally left it behind.

Miss Mass Transit

The angelic pipes behind the C-Train's automated stop announcements belong to Holly McConnell, the secretary to Calgary Transit's Superintendent of Operations. Back in '86, several CT employees were asked to submit demo tapes for the Teleride system (a.k.a. the bus-stop phone recordings telling you that the #10 just flew by while you were at home on the phone) and Holly won hands-down. The following year, she expanded her vocal empire by becoming the voice of the C-Train. In person, Holly doesn't sound half as chipmunky as she does on the train — blame sped-up cassette tape for her trademark pitch. Holly admits she "very rarely" rides the C-Train, insisting it's just the geographic reality of her daily commute and not the freakiness of hearing her modified voice repeatedly chirp "Erlton-Stampede!" and "You are now leaving the free fare zone!" As a testament to the enormity of her faceless celebrity, Alberta Theatre Projects once enlisted Holly to voice between-act stage announcements, complete with that annoying electronic bing-bong noise.

SLOW BOAT TO NOWHERE

It may not be the quickest way to get from A to B (or from A to A, in the case of a round-trip), but it's certainly not dull. The Lake Minnewanka Boat Tour (*762-3473*) has been in operation for some 25 years, offering a leisurely hour-and-a-half tour across the national park lake. During the ride, a guide points out all things Minnewanka: which mountain is which, locations seen in the Marilyn Monroe/Robert Mitchum pic *River of No Return*, and a multitude of wildlife beginning with the letter B (bats, big horn sheep, bald eagles). All that, *plus* the fact you're motoring overtop an entire sunken town, the dearly-departed Minnewanka Landing. It's kinda like your own personal sequel to *Deliverance*, but without hillbillies or Burt Reynolds.

Traffic Jams

Catch up on your knitting during one of these funtastic weekday traffic jams.

McKnight Blvd.

(between 19th St. NE and Centre St., afternoon)
Starts backing up around 3 p.m. and doesn't let up for a good four hours. Oddly enough, mornings aren't so bad.

Glenmore Tr.

(eastbound, morning)
The Elbow Drive intersection (affectionately known as "!@#") keeps traffic backed up all the way to Crowchild Tr. Once through the madness, commuters then face an agonizing wait to get onto Deerfoot. A better option: sleep in.

Macleod Tr.

(morning and afternoon rush hours)
Anywhere south of Southland Dr. is a nightmare, but especially between Midlake/Shawnessy Blvd. and Anderson Rd. (The south-leg of the LRT is a good thing – except everyone *drives* to and from the Anderson station.)

Elbow Dr.

(north of Glenmore, morning and afternoon)
Basically just one big playground zone. Don't be a fool.

Photo: Blaine Kyllo

Please Return Trays to Upright Position

From the Calgary aviation folklore files: an American pilot, having consulted an outdated map, was preparing to land on an extinct SW airstrip (now Mount Royal College). He made radio contact with the control tower at the Calgary International Airport, who mistakenly identified him as *another* airplane in the airport's vicinity. The control tower proceeded to give the pilot landing directions based on this second plane's position. You can imagine the ensuing zaniness: the control tower says one thing, the second airplane doesn't follow the directions, and halfway across town, the American pilot is thinking "All I see are trees." The pilot eventually crashed into a house, startling a woman doing dishes in the kitchen. Nobody was hurt, and everyone had a good laugh. (Actually, I'm not so sure about that "good laugh" part; the woman's house was pretty messed-up.)

Built for Speed (more or less)

In a sprawling burg like Calgary, the term "short cut" is a cruel joke, but a few routes will keep you on the move while the rest of the city is sucking exhaust on Macleod Trail.

Sarcee Tr.

"Speedy" is the word between the TransCan and 37th St. SW, but be careful around the Signal Hill/Westhills retail behemoth. Those must-turn right-hand lanes are unforgiving – once within the gravitational pull of the outlet stores, the laws of the universe will compel you to shop.

Centre St.

The rush hour lane-reversals really keep things moving, as long as you're going with the flow. That is, only the vehicularly perverted would venture *into* downtown during the afternoon. Avoid the left-hand turn lanes onto 16th Ave. (northbound) and into Chinatown (southbound). Of course, none of this means diddly-squat while the bridge is closed for repairs.

Photo: Blaine Kyllo

Edmonton Tr.

A good back-door into the downtown or onto Memorial Dr. (Again, all bets are off when the Centre St. bridge is closed.)

Crowchild Tr.

Who knows why, but the road's NW stretch really moves during the morning crunch. As for the afternoon . . . er, not so much.

Stoney Tr.

Smooth sailing between Crowchild Tr. and the TransCan, and a boffo alternative to cutting thru the endless playground zone that is Bowness. Nice view, too.

To avoid further aerial shenanigans, here are the locations of the area's legit landing strips and heliports:

Calgary International Airport

51°6'50" N / 114°01'13" W

Okotoks Airport

50°44" N / 113°56" W

Springbank Airport

51°6'11" N / 114°22'28" W

Requiem for the Rocketeer

Sometimes the future sounds really cool, but then it finally arrives and it's an overwhelming disappointment. Case in point: the Bell Aerosystems "Rocket Belt." Later seen in *Thunderball*, the Rocket Belt made its Canadian exhibition debut at the 1963 Calgary Stampede. Fairgoers were wowed by the up 'n' down antics of various Rocket Men as they soared high above the Stampede grounds. Imagine the excitement (finally: flashy fashion and speedy transportation, rolled into one!), then fast-forward thirtysomething years: are cargo pants really the best we can do?

Photo: Glenbow Archives NA 2864-181313-8

Speed Demons

Statistical nitpickers cheerily claim you're more likely to get in a car accident in the Chinook Centre parking lot, but everyone fears the Calf Robe Bridge all the same. True, the bridge has seen its share of horror, but why single out that particular stretch of Deerfoot Trail? Maybe it's the S-shaped design, throwing uncharacteristically sharp curves into the straight-ahead freeway. Maybe it's the proximity to the Bow River and Bonnybrook waste-treatment plant, a steamy combo conducive to heavy icing. Maybe its the *autobahn*esque speed limit. Or maybe it's something not of this world. In 1992, Siksika Nation Elders burned sweetgrass and buried tobacco under the Calf Robe Bridge. The following year, the number of accidents was cut in half. Spooky, no?

Airdrie Airport
51°15'50" N / 113°56'06" W

Prince's Island (heliport, not actually on the Island)
51°3'11" N / 114°04'43" W

Foothills Hospital (heliport)
51°3'52" N / 114°8'12" " W

Rockyview General Hospital (heliport)
50°59'20" N / 114°05'52" W

Alberta Children's Hospital (heliport)
51°2'14" N / 114°6'44" W

The Road King Truck Stop (*4949 Barlow Tr. SE*) is the best reason to double-clutch since that C.W. McCall song. A self-contained convenience wonderland, the 'King features an automated truckwash, Shifters Restaurant (good grub, terrible coffee, and they bring you an ashtray whether you want one or not), a motel, the 18 Wheeler's Lounge, a barbershop, and the Phantom 309 Games Room. Particularly entertaining is McCully's General Store, piled to the rafters with leather ball caps, T-shirts ("Truckers Are Good For The Long Haul"), bumper stickers, skin-mags, auto parts, and this weird battery-operated device which shrieks obscenities. Best value: two bucks for "Ginseng Blast," a 100 percent natural pick-me-up for those blacktop all-nighters.

Bow-Crow (heliport, west of city limits on north bank of Bow River)

51°6'10" N / 114°12'52" W

Westport (heliport)

51°2'12" N / 114°11'44E

Peter Lougheed Centre (heliport)

Decertified, so don't even think about it.

Caddie Shack

Nothing says "classy" like a pink '59 Caddie convertible with Elvis mural – except a pink '59 Caddie convertible with Elvis mural driven by an off-duty dairy farmer. Located just outside of Beiseker, the Cadillac Ranch (*947-2078*) is just what it sounds like: a bunch of old cars sitting on a farm. In addition to the ElvisMobile, there's a whack of Caddie convertibles (a blue 1960, a white '65 with neon pink and black interior, a red-pink '69) plus a maroon '74 Buick convertible, a '58 Chevy Impala sports coupe, and a two-door '77 Lincoln town coupe. And they're all for rent. Price varies according to how long you want them and how far you're going, but one thing is constant: Doug Straub is part of the deal. Weddings, graduations, retirement parties – whatever the occasion, Doug will stomp in from the fields, slip into a suit, and chauffeur you around. When things get busy, Doug's wife also takes the wheel.

Putting the "COP" in Helicopter

An infrared eye in the midnight sky, the police dept.'s HAWC 1 patrols the city like something straight outta *Blue Thunder*. (But unlike the *Blue Thunder* television show, HAWC 1 doesn't enjoy the luxury of Bubba Smith and Dick Butkus providing ground support.) What downtown citizen hasn't enjoyed the *X-Files*-esque experience of waking up to the peeping-tom glare of HAWC's Spectrolab SX16 searchlight? As for the trademark "pudda-pudda" sound, chalk it up to the McDonnell Douglas MD520N's lack of a tail rotor. (Chopper lingo calls the feature "NOTAR," and it cuts noise by 40 percent.) Finally, a science experiment: if you're out and about during the wee hours and HAWC 1 flies overhead, cast a nervous look skyward then run like hell. According to rumour, the air-crew will assume you're a nogoodnik and give chase. (Weasely disclaimer: I assume no responsibility for any mishaps occurring from such a childish stunt. Nor will I pony up bail, so don't waste your phone call.)

Photo: Blaine Kyllo

Top 10 Most Dangerous Intersections

The following 1998 accident statistics come courtesy of the Calgary Police Service's Traffic Section. Disclaimer: these numbers reflect frequency of traffic accidents and don't take into account traffic volume through that particular intersection. (It stands to reason that the busier the road, the more accidents.) Finally — and I've always wanted to say this — let's be careful out there.

Deerfoot Tr. and 16th Ave. NE
Number of accidents in 1998: 251

Deerfoot Tr. and Memorial Dr. NE
Number of accidents: 211

Deerfoot Tr. and Glenmore Tr. SE
Number of accidents: 197

Crowchild Tr. and Glenmore Tr. SW
Number of accidents: 142

Deerfoot Tr. and 17th Ave. SE
Number of accidents: 123

16th Ave. and 19th St. NE
Number of accidents: 113

**Anderson Rd. and
Macleod Tr. S**
Number of accidents: 109

Deerfoot Tr. and Peigan Tr. SE
Number of accidents: 103

Glenmore Tr. and 14th St. SW
Number of accidents: 99

**Macleod Tr. and
Southland Dr. S**
Number of accidents: 92

I Brake for Nato

Maybe it's a mountain thing, but there are a lot of "off-road" suburban command vehicles tooling around town. (It seems kinda unnecessary – then again, the Starbuck's parking lot can get pretty hairy sometimes.) Since the jeep was invented by the U.S. Army, the logical next step in 4x4 commuting is 55 tonnes of missile-resistant steel. For a mere $499 (plus GST, meals included), "Armor: The Ultimate Adventure Inc." (*229-4224*) will teach you how to drive a tank. The 10-hour course runs on weekends (June through October) and gives students hands-on experience with a Lynx Reconnaissance Vehicle (7 tonnes), an M113A2 (9 tonnes), and the aforementioned 55-ton big boy Chieftain MK11 Main Battle Tank. The course covers parallel parking, the proper negotiation of traffic circles, and how to crush things.

A Vote for Me is a Vote for Gridlock

Northbound 14th St. SW is easily, ridiculously sabotaged: all it takes is one stalled car (or overturned applecart, stray deer, etc.) on the Glenmore causeway and you're looking at instantaneous gridlock. "Why?" you may find yourself yelling into your no-spill coffee mug. "Why, lord, why?" The next time you're stuck on 14th, take a gander to the north. On a clear day, you can make out the northern stretch of 14th St., which looks like it would connect quite nicely to the rest of the street. (Gee, *there's* an idea.) In fact, 14th St. was originally intended to be a major, uninterrupted north-south artery. Why the bizarre reservoir detour, then? It seems a certain mayor lived in Mayfair/Bel-Aire, and he wasn't so keen on sacrificing his house to the commuter gods. Obviously well-versed in "don't bite the hand" theory (that is, what's the good of a commuter speedway when you're suddenly unemployed?), city council ixnayed the 14th St. extension back in the '60s – food for thought while you're idling away hours of your life overtop the reservoir's lovely waters.

Goodyear Eat Yer Heart Out

During the early '70s, Calgary held the distinction of being "The Hot-Air Balloon Capital of Canada." Several factors contributed to the sport's overwhelming popularity: close proximity to the mountains shielded the city from heavy winds, making for the light, breezy conditions conducive to ballooning; the sheer enthusiasm of a handful of balloonists; and the simple fact that balloons are allowed to fly over the city (not the case in, say, Toronto), thus generating excitement amongst the hoi polloi below. (I'm told we look like ants.) The city's title has long since been transferred to points east (always stealing our good ideas, ain't they?) and changes in global weather patterns have made for heavier winds, but there's still a whole lot of ballooning going on. Hot-air balloons land pretty much wherever they can, but 99% of 'em take off from the same place: the Museum of the Regiments *(4520 Crowchild Tr. S)*. Less-used second-string locales include a Richmond Green ball diamond, the Glenmore Spillway, a field belonging to the West Hillhurst Community Association, and South Glenmore Park.

Come Fly the Fancy Skies

For a cool $130,000, Sun West Home Aviation (275-8121) will fly you and seven of your closest friends to Japan onboard a luxurious Hawker 800, leave the motor running while you pop out for sushi, and then whisk you back to Calgary International Airport. Those on a more modest travel budget may wish to make the round-trip via Lear jet, for a mere $90G. The Lear only seats six people, and it's more cramped than the Hawker (no full-service galley, either), but such is poverty. For shorter flights, Sun West offers spins in a fully-restored 1942 Stearman biplane. It won't get ya to Japan, but the biplane can handle barrel-rolls and all that other barnstorming trickery. $300/hour gets you the plane and a pilot.

MORE Secret Tunnels

Alyth Railyards
At the end of Alyth Rd. SE, just past the "Thank God I'm An Athiast" [sic] graffiti, a one-lane tunnel takes cars underneath the train tracks and back up into the heart of the railyard. It's a convenience thing, allowing yard access even when the tracks are jammed with trains. Traffic lights, timed at two-minute intervals, prevent head-on collisions in the skinny passage. It's a quick ride, and there's not much to see on either side unless you *really* like trains, but it's still kinda cool.

City Hall LRT
A concealed ladder descends from the alderman's level of the City Hall parkade into an unused 150-metre LRT tunnel. Empty for over fifteen years, the tunnel awaits a future (and possibly never-to-be) LRT expansion which would divert the trains from 7th Ave. (above) to 8th Ave. (below). Regardless of whether the zillion-dollar idea ever comes to pass, planners decided it would be most cost-efficient to build the tunnel at the same time as

the Municipal Building. The next time you're riding in the southbound tunnel between the existing City Hall and Stampede stations, you may be able to sneak a fleeting peek at the secret tunnel's entrance.

Secret Lift

The Arts Centre is home to the only human-operated elevators in Western Canada. (By "human-operated," I mean there's someone who opens/closes the double-doors and controls where the elevator stops — not some breathless guy on a treadmill powering the whole operation.) The two elevators are located just inside the "Public Building" entrance next to the Jack Singer Concert Hall. The Public Building houses various arts organizations (CPO, PanCanadian WordFest, etc.) and an old-school top-floor cafeteria, in case you're looking for an excuse to ride.

As for the whole "Public Building" biz, that's a hold-out from the building's past lives as a jail and post office. Workers recently discovered deep grooves worn into the Jack Singer "Founders Room" floor, a souvenir from the days when people lined up to buy stamps and mail their tax returns. There's still a jail cell in the sub-basement, too.

The Inglewood-Vegas Car Connection

At Farmer Jones Used Carz, democracy is job one. (Spelling is a distant second.) For almost 50 years, the car lot has turned a blind eye to bad credit, offering easy-care financing to Joe/Josephete LunchPail. (Carz run as low as $200. That's not $200/month, that's $200 *period*.) But what of the good farmer himself? Edward "Farmer Jones" Pizinger's mother died in the Saskatchewan flu epidemic of 1918, so the youngster was sent to live with a Nebraskan uncle. Pizinger grew up to own a new car dealership in Nevada during the early days of Las Vegas, selling wheels to Bugsy Siegel ("You didn't have to worry about getting your money" when dealing with gangsters, he says) and chumming around with Abbott and Costello at the Flamingo Hotel. (Pizinger credits health food with his having outlived his Vegas cronies. But not ticking off the Mob couldn't have hurt.) Tiring of desert life, Farmer J. traded some Vegas property for a swank house in Inglewood (Los Angeles), which eventually led him to Portland, and finally to his current roost in Inglewood (Calgary). He was actually en route to Edmonton, but he liked the cut of Calgary's jib. The rest, as they say, is a bunch of exhaust-stained stuffed animals propping open the hoods of cars.

If you're looking for secret Bow River fishin' holes, don't hold your breath.
(I tried. Oh, how I tried. But those anglers are a tight-lipped bunch,
consarnit!) If, on the other hand, you're in the mood for man-made lakes,
nudity (both drunken and family-approved), toboggan hills,
and pro wrestling – read on.

the hustler

Now retired – save for the occasional exhibition game – Joe Big Plume started hustling pool before age twenty. By the late 1940s he was pocketing $40 a day, and once earned $3,500 after a grueling seven-hour game. Big Plume won several provincial snooker championships and often placed high in national tournaments. But he clinched his legend status during a 1970s exhibition game in Calgary, mopping the felt with none other than Minnesota Fats.

ring-a-ding-dong daddy

He's best known as the premier's pa, but during the '50s Phil Klein wrestled under various *noms-de-mat,* including "The Phantom," "The Mask," and the less-than-terrifying "Logger Felix." According to one source, Klein Sr.'s trademark manoeuvre was a piledriver followed by an off-the-top-rope hospital closure. (Just kidding, Felix.)

Bacchus in the Saddle Again

The Cowtown Saddle Company Rodeo has built a reputation for quality debauchery. The name and location have changed over the event's twenty-plus history, but that's of little import since everyone just calls it "that rodeo where drunk people run around naked." Held on the first Saturday of Stampede, the organizers refer to the CSCR as "our personal Stampede party with 1,000 of our closest friends." Partygoers pay big coin to be bused outside the city for a day of food, fun, and non-stop booze. (The average year yields a $27,000 bar tab.) Guests partake in four traditional rodeo events (e.g. the calf-scramble), but it's #5 which gets tongues a-waggin': Truth Or Dare. Basically a relay race with a beer incentive, Truth Or Dare always ends with nakedness. Always. Always. *Always.*

A steak dinner follows the flesh parade, after which everyone enjoys a slide show of the day's blurry events. Lest ye think the CSCR signals the end of civilization, you should know that the whole shebang is a fundraiser for children's charities. Drunken nakedness with a conscience – what a concept.

Secret Speedo View

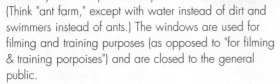

The University of Calgary's Aquatic Centre has underwater observation windows which offer a shark's-eye-view of pool activity. (Think "ant farm," except with water instead of dirt and swimmers instead of ants.) The windows are used for filming and training purposes (as opposed to "for filming & training porpoises") and are closed to the general public.

Toboggan Hills

Our tundra-locked friends to the North may have two zillion different words for *snow*, but only one for *insanity*: toboggan. Local toboggan daredevils whisper about stolen moments in the Shaganappi Golf Course, but there's lots of hi-speed alternatives for the less trespassing inclined. Those with an insatiable jones for rocketing downhill on slippery wood are directed to the following hills:

Confederation Park (NW)
14th St. and 31st Ave. NW

Deerfoot Athletic Park (NE)
east of Deerfoot Tr., between 8th Ave. and 16th Ave. NE

Pop Davies Athletic Park (SE)
Millican Rd. and Ogden Rd. SE

Prairie Winds Park (NE)
40th St. and 54th Ave. NE

That big hill in St. Andrews Heights, just off University Dr. (NW)

Outdoorsy Groups

Alberta Speleological Society
Dedicated to the exploration/conservation of caves, members hike around looking for, well, caves. Collectively, they've discovered and mapped 100 caves in the province. Annual membership: $15.
Phone: 245-8823.

Bow Waters Canoe Club
The club runs several white-water canoeing tours, ranging from novice to "crazy-stupid." In the winter, the BWCC's fancy turns to Nordic skiing and telemarking. Annual membership: $40/single, $55/family.
Phone: 235-2922.

Calgary Balloon Club
Founded in 1976, the club owns three hot-air balloons. Pilot members get to fly the balloons, everyone else gets to act as a crew. Club meetings are held every second Wednesday (September to June) at the Aerospace Museum, 7:30 pm. Annual membership: $35.
Phone: 240-1491.

Calgary Mountain Bike Alliance
The CMBA can hook you up with local riding groups, and offers info on environmentally/socially responsible off-road biking. *Phone: 220-1868.*

Stampede Wrestling

Good luck explaining it to the peach-fuzzed teen sporting an "Austin 3:16" T-shirt, but today's pro-wrestling explosion wouldn't even be a whimper were it not for Stampede Wrestling. In 1930, a 98-lb Edmonton weakling named Stu Hart entered the world of traditional keep-it-on-the-mat wrestling. He quickly ascended to the top of the sport and was considered a no-problemo for Olympic gold. World War II scuttled those dreams, however, and Hart moved to Calgary where he turned his talents toward professional wrasslin'.

During its 40-year history, Stu Hart's Stampede Wrestling shaped a tonne of major talent who would go on to join bigger, higher-profile leagues: Gene Kiniski, Whipper Billy Watson, Abdullah The Butcher, Chris Benoit, "Killer" Tor Kamata, Big Daddy Ritter (a.k.a Junkyard Dog), Davey Boy Smith, Dynamite Kid, Andre The Giant, Jim "The Anvil" Neidhart, Jake "The Snake" Roberts, Bastion Booger (a.k.a. Norman the Lunatic, a.k.a. Makhan Singh, a.k.a. Mike Shaw), the HonkyTonk Man (né HonkyTonk Wayne), as well as Stu's own flesh and blood, Bret The Hitman and Owen.

Disillusioned with the industry's increasing reliance on soap opera shenanigans, Stu Hart shut down Stampede Wrestling in 1989. (Television reruns, complete with Ed Whalen's patented "malfunction at the junction" commentary, are in circulation around the world. One little problem: they're all illegal bootlegs.) The Hart Family revived the franchise in 1999 to counteract the sex-sells approach of Vince McMahon's gimmick-happy WWF. The new Stampede Wrestling may not be as squeaky-clean as it likes to think (witness the "Stampede Wrestling Kicks Ass" T-shirts and the jiggling ringside presence of Hooters girls), but there's no denying that a Hart-trained grappler sure knows how to wrestle.

Stu Hart's quest to restore pro-wrestling to its former glory took on tragic new relevance when, mere weeks after Stampede Wrestling's return, his son Owen was killed in a ridiculous WWF stunt gone horribly wrong. In attendance at Owen Hart's funeral was a veritable who's-who of pro-wrestling, and his Queens Park grave attracts mourners from around the world.

what backswing?

Disc golf has been around for decades, but it's only caught fire locally in the past ten years. Definitely not as "corporate" as its clubs 'n' balls cousin, disc golf is a very casual affair (not a lot of business deals go down on the disc course).

The general idea is pretty much like traditional golf: throw your disc into the hole, except the hole is a metal cage basket thingie. Discs vary in sizes and weights according to purpose: driving, chipping, or putting. The disc acts as both club and ball . . . er, unless your arm is considered the club . . . then again, you also use your arms in regular golf so . . . ah, forget it. (One definite difference from "normal" golf: the courses are free.)

The curious should consult the Alberta Disc Sports Association newsletter (*Huck*), available at Bow Cycle Sports and Lifesport.

There are various proposals floating about, but so far only two established courses in/near Calgary:

Pearce Estate Park

There are 18 permanent holes, nine in the main park, nine on the other side of the overflow creek. The park is also popular for outdoor weddings, which can make for some weird scenes. (Pearce Estate is in Inglewood; drive north on 17A St. SE from 17th Ave. and you can't miss it.)

Canmore Nordic Centre

The 18-hole permanent course was set up five years ago, and recently upgraded with brand new baskets. The first tee starts near the biathlon grandstand. The Canmore Nordic Centre is located at 1988 Olympic Way in, you guessed it, Canmore. (Don't know if disc golf is exactly what Ancient Greece meant by "Olympic legacy," but. . . .)

Bocce

Yeah, it's basically old people rolling balls — but if you think bocce is the same as lawn bowling, you've got another thing comin', bambino.

Calgary Italian Club (indoor)
416-1st Ave. NE, 264-4133

Croatian Canadian Cultural Centre (outdoor)
3010-12th St. NE, 250-9821

Our Lady of Grace Italian & English Church (indoor)
1714-14th Ave. NE, 276-1689

Thorncliff Greenview Community Centre (outdoor)
5600 Centre St. N, 274-5574

Lawn Bowling

There's something strangely soothing about watching lawn bowling, kinda like staring at a fish tank. (I know they're now calling the sport "bowls," but "lawn bowling" just has a certain ring to it.) Maybe it's the smooth graceful motion, maybe it's the clothes. Decide for yourself.

Bow Valley Lawn Bowling Club
1738 Bowness Rd. NW, 270-2862

Calgary Lawn Bowling Club
1238-16th Ave. SW, 245-4341

Inglewood Lawn Bowling Club
1235-8th Ave. SE, 263-1769

Dungeons & Armdrags

ANDRE THE GIANT

Some kids fear the basement because of imaginary monsters, others just don't want to get bodyslammed. Nicknamed "The Dungeon," the basement of Stu Hart's home has churned out generations of pro wrestlers. (Not surprisingly, all his kids either wrestled or married wrestlers.) Today, sons Bruce & Ross carry on the Dungeon legacy with the Hart Brothers Training Camp. Still held in Stu's basement, the school runs three days a week, three hours a day. As far as post-grad job placement goes, the Dungeon boasts a better track-record than DeVry: aside from the Hart boys and several ex-Stampeders – the football team, not those "Sweet City Woman" wimps – alumni include Chris Benoit, Hiro Hase, Gerry Albright, and Phil Lafon. Coursework covers offensive and counter moves, how to fall, conditioning, endurance, and weightlifting. The Stampede Wrestling patriarch himself even pops by to give demonstrations on rendering your opponent a harmless sack of jelly using pressure points. Would-be tough-guys are advised to write the camp. *727, 105-150 Crowfoot Cres. NW, T3G 3T2.*

Them Bones

There's debate as to whether the Sunnyside embankment was an actual buffalo jump, or just an enormous buffalo slaughtering ground. (Bet you never thought you'd hear the words ". . . just an enormous buffalo slaughtering ground," huh?) Either way, there were so many darn bones lying around that Sunnysideans circa 1910 decorated their white picket fences with sun-bleached skulls. To this day, Sunnyside has a relatively low occurrence of home break-ins. Me, I'll take a skull over a fake "Protected by Spurious Alarm Systems Inc." sticker any day.

public sex

Alderman Barry Erskine caused a stink when he demanded the police HAWC helicopter be used to root out homosexual hanky-panky in North Glenmore Park. Hey, some people like satin sheets & candlelight, others enjoy romping in the great outdoors. So while the Erskmeister busies himself in the bushes with a flashlight and butterfly net, consider taking a field trip with that special someone. Oh, the thrill of it all.

Nose Hill

This place is big, offering sex under the stars with little chance of discovery. Bring a blanket, and keep one eye open for witches and curious dogs.

University of Calgary sub-levels

Photo: Sven Schwinn

Some science building stairwells descend an extra level past the basement, making the ideal location for a li'l between-class cram session between you and a study partner. Allow for the possibility of a startled custodian.

University of Calgary Climbing Wall

It's an unsupervised wall, and amorous climbers have been known to rendezvous at the summit. Doesn't chalk cause chafing? Guess not.

Devonian Gardens

Not private at all, but there's something about fountains that brings out the beast in some people. At least move away from the glass elevator, perv.

Mini-Golf

The smell of freshly-cut artificial grass mingles with go-kart exhaust and gas fumes. You quiver in anticipation. For those about to ricochet off the windmill, we salute you.

Kart Gardens
9555 Barlow Tr. NE, 250-9555

Prairie Winds
333 Castleridge Blvd. NE, 285-7770

Target Greens
1851-184th St. NE, 285-2009

Paskapoo Greens
Canada Olympic Park, 247-5452

Kart World
5202-1st St. SW, 253-8301

Tee To Green
Macleod Tr. & Shawnessy Blvd. SW, 256-7447

Bowness Park
8900-48th Ave. NW, 286-9889

Drive (and Putt), She Said

When Colonel James Macleod dubbed the N.W.M.P.'s new fort "Calgary," he mistakenly thought the word was Gaelic for "clear running water." Years later, scholars discovered the true definition: "clear running water with 18 holes and a driving range." No wonder Calgary is a super-huge golf city, the likes of which are rarely seen outside the bonny wee homeland. A cautionary tale: swingers wishing to join the Calgary Golf & Country Club (est. 1897) face an 18-year waiting list. Ach.

Corporate golf tournaments are as ubiquitous as pancakes during Stampede, so much so that people freely use phrases like "ball sponsor" without a trace of embarrassment. Not since typhoid has there been such a widely-accepted truancy excuse: "Ooooh, no-go on the Monday meeting. I'm playing in the FakeName Inc. golf tournament. But I'll be back on Friday." A lovely walk ruined by a demonic little ball? Say what you will, but Calgarians have embraced the game of golf like Alice Cooper has embraced...uh, *golf*, I guess.

In 1938, a British civil servant named Albert Stephen Ignatius Gispert organized a cross-country run among fellow ex-pats living in Kuala Lumpur. Gispert based the runs on the cheery fun enjoyed by terrified rabbits and pursuing dogs. One runner (the "hare") would get a headstart, marking his trail with flour, chalk, ribbons, etc. (False trails add to the festivities.) The rest of the runners ("hounds") would pursue the hare. Afterward, hare and hounds alike would get blotto at the nearest watering hole. And so was born the Hash House Harriers. (As for the weird moniker, the group's post-run meeting place was nicknamed "the Hash House" because of its lousy food.)

After taking a WWII breather, hashing returned with a vengeance. Soon enough, the triple-H spread to Italy, Singapore, and beyond. There are now over 1,300 hashes worldwide, including five in Calgary: the original Calgary Hash House Harriers (Monday nights at 7 p.m.), Calgary Full Moon Hash (nighttime runs under, yes, a full moon), Calgary Only Goes Sometimes Bike Hash (mixes off- and on-road cycling), Rocky Mountain Hash House Harriers (biweekly, Saturday afternoons, fifty to ninety minute runs with mid-run beer break), and the Calgary Kid's Hash (kids & parents, first and third Sunday of the summer months).

The HHH calls itself "a drinking club with a running problem," and with good reason: after completing fifty runs, a Hasher earns the right to chug-a-lug 40 oz. of free beer. (Hashers stress the fun, non-competitive nature of their club. Duh.) Call 254-9014 to find out where/when the next run is, then just show up. (Don't leave a message 'cuz they won't listen to it.)

Hash House Huh?

As with any society worth its salt, lingo abounds in the Hash House Harriers. A sampling:

Hash : The run itself, in which "hounds" chase the "hare." Usually ends in drinking.

FRB : Short for "Front Running Bastard," the hasher who runs ahead of the pack and figures out the hare's true trail.

BOP : Short for "Back of the Pack."

Check (or Checking):

Indicates a fork in the trail. One choice leads to the hare and the beer. The other path is what's known as a "falsie."

Checkback:

Indicates the end of a falsie. Time to turn around, lest the hare empties the keg.

Down-Down:

The chugging of beer after a well-hashed hash.

Secret Migration

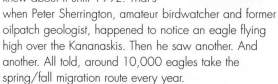

The Calgary region has been a major golden eagle migration spot for some 11,000 years, but nobody knew about it until 1992. That's when Peter Sherrington, amateur birdwatcher and former oilpatch geologist, happened to notice an eagle flying high over the Kananaskis. Then he saw another. And another. All told, around 10,000 eagles take the spring/fall migration route every year.

Don't quote me on it, but the whole deal has something to do with special thermal drafts which boost the birds high enough to fly over the Rockies. Once up, they keep on truckin' to summer homes in Alaska and the Yukon. (Some naturalists think the eagles fly as far as Siberia.) In the fall, the birds reverse the process as they return to winter in Wyoming, southern Montana, and eastern Colorado.

Bird-minded watchers travel from around the world to check out the migrations. Some of the best spots for catching eagle action are: Lake Minnewanka (west end), Gap Lake (near Seebe), Nakiska Lookout (Highway 40), Cougar Creek (Canmore), and Barrier Lake (Kananaskis Country). Those little fellas fly high and fast, so bring binoculars.

Different Strokes

The Different Strokes Calgary Swim Club is a great place for gays and lesbians to get wet. (That wasn't supposed to sound sordid, honest.) The group is not, I repeat not, a Gary Coleman appreciation society. The club meets at the Downtown YWCA (320-5th Ave. SE) on Sundays at 7 p.m. and Wednesdays at 6 p.m.

Confederation Park (city course)
3204 Collingwood Dr. NW, 974-1800
9 holes, 3221 yards, par 36

Country Hills
Beddington Tr. & Country Hills Blvd., 226-7777
9 holes public, 3500 yards, par 36

Douglasdale
7 Douglaswoods Dr. SE, 279-7913
18 holes, 4300 yards, par 60

Elks of Calgary
2502-6th St. NE, 276-5040
18 holes, 6500 yards, par 72

Fox Hollow
999-32nd Ave. NE, 277-4653
18 holes, 6500 yards, par 72

Heather Glen
100th St. & Glenmore Trail SE, 236-4653
18 holes, 6399 yards, par 72

Inglewood
34th Ave. & Barlow Tr. SE, 272-4363
18 holes, 6218 yards, par 71

Lakeview (city course)
5840-19th St. SW, 974-1815
9 holes, 1612 yards, par 30

Maple Ridge (city course)
1240 Mapleglade Dr. SE, 974-1825
18 holes, 6576 yards, par 72

McCall Lake (city course)
1600-32nd Ave. NE, 974-1805
27 holes, 6788 yards, par 71

Richmond Green (city course)
2539-33th Ave. SW, 974-1820
9 holes, 1214 yards, par 27

Shaganappi Point (city course)
1200-26th St. SW, 974-1810
27 holes, 5284 yards, par 69

Valley Ridge
11618 Valley Ridge Park NW, 288-9457
27 holes, 6642 yards, par 72

Flagpole Sitta

Dunno if it counts as a "sport" exactly, but Bill "The Human Spider" Strothers once climbed the Palliser Hotel's outer wall (10 stories), then shimmied to the top of the rooftop flagpole. Did I mention he was blindfolded the whole time? This was in 1921, when entertainment was apparently rather scarce, so 15,000 people gathered to watch The Spider do his thing. Curds and whey were served. (Do not try this at home, at least not until you've practiced on the water-spout.)

Sport of Kings

File under: who knew? The Calgary Polo Club, actually located in DeWinton, is the oldest polo club in Canada. Southern Albertan pony people first played polo (after picking packs of pickled peppers, naturally) in the early 1880s. The club itself debuted in 1890.

Sore (Really, *Really* Sore) Losers

Straight from the locker-room rumour mill: the University of Calgary rugby team supposedly folded after it stopped receiving tournament invitations. Why the sudden unpopularity? It seems the team was blessed with a bounty of foreign students (read: fun-loving Aussies), and the opposition grew tired of consistently being knocked senseless.

Martha Stewart Stinking

It's easy to take the Rocky Mountains for granted. Yeah, they're big. Yeah, they're old. Sometimes it takes an outsider's eyes to appreciate the beauty of our own backyard. An outsider like, say, Martha Stewart.

Stewart was reportedly paid $25,000 to attend "An Evening With Martha Stewart," a $175 a plate dinner in support of Autism Treatment Services of Canada. The day before the "evening with" was spent hiking around Banff, and the domestic powerhouse was so taken with the mountains that she couldn't bear to wash away the memories. Or comb her hair. She showed up at the Roundup Centre shockingly disheveled, ate some salad, then split for a private dinner in Chinatown. (Autism can be a real bummer, sure, but you'd think she could've at least boiled some buffalo-bones to make a nice lavender-ambrosia-coconut soap.) A roomful of "An Evening Without Martha Stewart" patrons were left to fume over their dessert, which I'm told was either roasted Italian plums with *créme fraiche* or frozen chocolate bars on paper plates.

Swing Low Sweet Euphemism

Founded in 1952, the Sunny Chinooks Association (*274-8166*) is Calgary's only nudist club. The group's 100-or-so members pay an annual $145 fee, entitling them to get *au naturel* at various year-round activities, such as winter swimming at a local indoor pool and summer fun at the SCA's very own campground. (Needless to say, the club won't divulge either location, but the secret camp is somewhere north of Calgary.) Sunny Chinookers are a family-oriented bunch who enjoy volleyball, basketball, and long walks in the woods. They take Lyme Disease and skin cancer very seriously, meaning their definition of "naked" includes sunblock and hats. "We're nudists," says a SCA spokesnudist. "We're not stupid."

Fake Lakes, Real Fish

In 1963, local construction baron E.V. Keith attended a Chicago housebuilding conference regarding the importance of selling "lifestyle" rather than just houses. (Note: "swingers" may refer to their swaptastic sex practices as "The Lifestyle," but I don't think that's what the Chicago convention was talking about.) Keith immediately revamped his plans for a new Calgary neighbourhood called Willow Park. One golf course later, the community "lifestyle" revolution was underway. In 1967, Keith checked out some L.A. developments built around manmade lakes. People called him crazy, but Lake Bonavista (1968) was not only Canada's first manmade lake community but the beginning of Calgary's love affair with unnatural bodies of water. (The ever-present waterfalls, by the way, aren't just decoration: they also oxygenate the water.) The lake communities are inherently "Calgary" on many levels: the flashy parade of big bucks (some lakefront homes fetch upwards of $700,000), the promotion of urban sprawl (originally concentrated in the SE nether-regions, lakes have recently popped up in the northern fringes), and the smalltown fear of big city livin' (although not gated-communities, there's definitely a "not in my backyard lake" vibe — non-residents are *non grata*). But the best reason is the simplest: the lakes are stocked with rainbow trout. Huge, dull-witted rainbow trout. Fishing is encouraged, *if* you live in the neighbourhood and aren't delinquent with your annual user fees. (Lake fees usually vary according to a home's proximity to water.) As for the rest of you, your best bet is to loiter around the front gates and try to make a new friend. (Possible tactics include: helping change a tire, feigning amnesia and suggesting a freshly-hooked trout will help shake the cobwebs, and good old-fashioned bribery.) Happy fishin', and don't mind the near-toxic levels of goose crap.

Lake Bonavista (SE)

Size: 52 acres

Max. depth: 26 feet

Annual lake fees: $130

Lake Midnapore (SE)

Size: 30 acres

Max. depth: 35 feet

Annual lake fees: $160

Bonus fish: yellow perch

Swiss Misters

In 1896, a vacationing Boston lawyer rolled 300 metres down the icy slope of Mt. Lefroy. The fatal accident prompted Canadian Pacific Railways to import genuine Swiss mountain guides. (After all, if the railroad was transporting all those rich would-be adventurers into the mountains, the least they could do was make sure they stayed alive long enough to spend more money.)

CPR halted its Swiss guide programme in 1955, but several of the climbers remained in the area. Bruno Engler, for example, went on to become a renowned photographer and Sunshine's first ski instructor. (That was back when Sunshine was just a CPR rest-area for hikers en route to Mt. Assiniboine.) His mug also graces the label of a Bow Valley Brewing Company beer, as well as Bruno's Café & Grill in Banff.

Finally, a sartorial note: to lend an air of old-country professionalism, the Swiss guides wore quaint outfits (ties, leather boots, traditional woolen suits) that are radically different from the fleecy Mountain Equipment Co-op look favoured by today's climbers. Contemporary dope activists, however, will be pleased to learn that the Swiss guides used hemp rope.

Cruel & Unusual Shoes

Now let us praise famous wrestling boot manufacturers. (As Ed Whalen would surely attest, the phrase "taking the boots to him" wouldn't make a heckuva lotta sense if wrestlers fought barefoot.) Once upon a time, the walls of Kingsland Shoe Repairs *(7732 Elbow Dr. SW)* were jammed with autographed pictures of the store's pro wrestling clientele. The guy behind the counter says the shop no longer makes customized wrasslin' boots, and he can't remember who bought the things anyway. (So much for celebrity endorsements.) Maybe his elves handled all the wrestling accounts. Anyway, the old photos are packed away in a box, but the shoemaker hopes to get new pics: "My kids like wrestling."

Hey Boo-Boo: It's a Pic-a-Nic Basket

There's no shortage of out-of-town picnic getaways, it's finding the time to vamoose the city limits that can be a bugger. Fortunately, Calgary is blessed with mucho green space, making it apple-pie easy to transform an extended lunch hour into an urban picnic. Some suggested destinations, both gritty and grassy:

Edworthy Park

Enter from the south (up the hill in Spruce Cliff) or the north (at the Shaganappi/Memorial intersection). The main park is good for a dog-and-frisbee vibe, while the dense westbound trails offer a quick-fix for that bizarre, quintessentially Calgary feeling: you know you're in the city, but all you can see is trees. (If you root around the fields near the traintracks, you can see the faint remains of the Brickburn factory, which cranked out 45,000 bricks a day during the 1920s.)

Carburn Park

Hidden in the southwest corner of Riverside, Carburn Park features two manmade lakes stocked with yellow perch and northern pike. Plenty o' tables and shelters and firepits make this a civilized wilderness retreat.

Peter's Drive-In

A chocolate-banana shake, a cheeseburger with that weird extra half patty, and thou. All that, plus divebombing gulls and the oily rumble of the TransCan. *Très romantique, non?*

Lake Sundance (SE)
Size: 35 acres
Max. depth: 38 feet
Annual lake fees: $185-260

Arbour Lake (NW)
Size: 10 acres
Max. depth: 19 feet
Annual lake fees: $186-$372
Bonus fish: Arctic char, brook trout

Lake Chaparral (SE)
Size: 33 acres
Max. depth: 40 feet
Annual lake fees: $230-$353

Weaselhead Flats

The polar opposite of Peter's. A short stroll into the west-end of Glenmore Park (at the southern tip of Lakeview) and you're surrounded by pines, willows, birds, and maybe even deer. Not a lot of benches, so bring a blanket.

Sandy Beach

Speaking of blankets, Sandy Beach isn't just for late-night winky-wink; it's also an A-1 destination for riverside picnicking. (Access the park via 50th Ave and 14A St. SW.) Noon-hour bonus: you can inner-tube back to work, provided you don't mind portaging from Fort Calgary into downtown.

Calgary International Airport

OK, not exactly at the airport, but darn close. Airport observation decks were nixed in the early '70s (breach of security and all), and replaced with off-site viewing parks: turn off McCall Way NE near Runway 28, pull up a picnic table, and watch the planes come and go. Just like the opening scene of *Easy Rider*, but with egg-salad.

Coral Springs Lake (NE)

Size: 16 acres

Max. depth: 25 feet

Annual lake fees: $250-$500

McKenzie Lake (SE)

Size: 43 acres

Max. depth: 28 feet

Annual lake fees: $262-$535

Lake Bonaventure (SE)

Size: 35 acres

Max. depth: 30 feet

Annual lake fees: $800

Fun fact: Unlike other manmades, Bonaventure is off-limits to almost all but lakeside residents.

Bonus fish: suckers

Wright Does Wrong

Photo: Courtesy of the Whyte Museum of the Canadian Rockies

Frank Lloyd Wright's architectural career briefly hit the skids during the 1910s (there's just something about leaving your family to run off with a client's wife that doesn't sit well with people), so he jumped at the Canadian government's offer to design the Banff National Park Pavilion.

As Canada's first national park began to grow, residents clamored for a covered hockey/curling rink. The government tired of the whining, and commissioned Wright to build an open-air pavilion. Anyone familiar with the concept of winter will realize the limited appeal of such a structure. The good people of Banff were cheesed because the long 'n' low building (completed in 1913) was exactly what they didn't want: three large rooms, each complete with its own huge fireplace, and nary an ice rink to be found. (Wright's River Forest Tennis Club in Illinois is the Banff Pavilion's kissin' cousin, design-wise.) The locals grew ever-more restless upon learning of the Pavilion's then-outrageous $20,000 price-tag. The final blow was the building's location. Cleverly constructed on a flood plain, the Pavilion was not only regularly submerged under water (adios, hardwood floors!) but swamp-like conditions made the place ground zero for mosquitoes.

After 25 years of near-constant disrepair, the controversial building was finally levelled. 'Tis a pity: Wright drafted a mere handful of Canadian projects (including a never-realized Banff railroad station) and the Pavilion was one of only two designs built to his exact specs. The other, a cottage on Ontario's Sapper Island, is still standing. (On the other hand, the Pavilion pretty much sucked.)

A handful of Wright champions hope to one day rebuild his Rocky Mountain masterpiece. Until then, you can remember ol' Frank Lloyd with a memorial soccer game at the Pavilion's former site. (From Banff Ave., turn west onto Cave Ave. Hang a right onto Sundance Rd. just past the Luxton Museum. Not much to see except grass and elk, but them's the breaks.)

MORE Outdoorsy Types

Alpine Club of Canada – Calgary
283-7657

Bow River Chapter Trout Unlimited
278-7370

Calgary Archers Club
259-5505

Calgary Beach Volleyball Association
691-7666

Calgary District Cricket League
271-5448

Calgary Field Naturalists Society
285-8553

You Can't Get to Heaven on Rollerblades

Golden in theory, tarnished in practice: The Sheldon Kennedy Foundation was a charity only a mother could love. True, the key points in Shel's hardluck story occurred elsewhere (abuse in Saskatchewan, the glug-glug-vroom-vroom Hummer incident in Edmonton, the ill-fated dream ranch in B.C.), but Calgary is still proud to call the lovable screw-up our own. After the Foundation nixed the B.C. ranch and donated its remaining money to the Red Cross, our hockey-haired "hero" defended his outrageous $65,000 paycheque with endearing hoser-speak: "If anyone else wants to strap on the skates and travel across the country for no money . . . they can have at 'er." Shine on, you kooky diamond.

Calgary RoadRunners

541-1498

Elbow Valley Cycle Club

283-BIKE

Foothills Nordic Ski Club

247-9572

Hook and Hackle Club

547-8995

Hostel Outdoors Group

283-5551

Petroleum City Ski and Social Club

269-6591

Rocky Mountain Ramblers

282-6308

The Island Formerly Known as Peninsula

The Alberta Hotel was named after Queen Victoria's daughter (long before our fair province was so crowned, no less), but Prince's Island has absolutely *nothing* to do with any fancy-pants princes. Heck, it's not even an island. When lumber magnate Peter Prince took over a downtown lumber mill in 1886, he needed a water channel with which to divert logs from the Bow River. (Prince showed up on the scene in 1886. The 1886 Café occupies the old Eau Claire Lumber Co. office. D'ya see how it's all coming together?) A little dynamite here 'n' there, and presto! Prince transformed a ho-hum peninsula into an exciting island. And so, history fans, Mr. Peter Prince is the reason it's so hard to sneak into the Folk Festival.

Photo: Blaine Kyllo

The Stampede breakfast is like cowboy Halloween: you dress up, walk around, and strangers give you free food. Heck, you don't even have to dress up. (Witness the proliferation of the downtown lazyman's Western look: jeans & tucked-in dress shirt. Way to go, Hoss.) There are hundreds of free Stampede breakfasts every year, and it's possible to hit a half-dozen of 'em on any given morning without breaking a sweat or cracking a map. Cramping, however, is a whole other story.

(As a side note, one of the weirdest Stampede breakfasts is a church-sponsored event held on the Ranchman's patio. It doesn't get more bizarre than a pancake-fueled sermon on the evils of drinking, delivered overtop the buzz of a neon Budweiser sign.)

I'm not knocking the traditional shopping mall parking-lot breakfast (pancakes, some sort of pork product, juice, coffee – plus weird entertainment like a Swedish brass band or spunky dogs), but the best spreads are found at corporate functions. To the dutiful employee, the company breakfast is The Man's way of saying "Thanks for working hard all year. Kick back, enjoy a champagne and OJ, and then get back to work before 9." To the gutsy cheapskate, it's free booze (and maybe eggs) without the burden of actually having to hold a job.

Don't let the fact that you're not an employee prevent you from scoring breakfast. Don't expect a successful infiltration every time, and prepare for the embarrassment of being busted, but corporate breakfasts *are* crashable. As with any deception, the key is to look like you're supposed to be there. Don't waffle near the entrance; barge right up to the greeting table and fill out a nametag. In fact, the nametag is your greatest weapon. Devise a pseudonym heavy with consecutive consonant clusters; clumsy attempts to pronounce your

Thanks For Coming Out

Barbershop scuttlebutt has both the Flames and Cannons packing their bags for warmer climes, and the Stamps – well, bless their pigskin hearts. In these times of turmoil, let us bow our heads in remembrance of the city's dearly-departed sports teams.

Basketball

We won't even get into the utter lameness of calling a sports team The Calgary 88s (what, was "The Volunteers" already taken?). At any rate, the World Basketball League died a quick death – but not as quick as the six-team National Basketball League, which folded in '94 mere months after the Calgary Outlaws joined its ranks.

Hockey

The World Hockey Association was launched in 1972 as an NHL rival, and crumbled seven years later when four of its teams (Edmonton, Winnipeg, Hartford, Quebec) jumped ship. The Calgary Cowboys weren't so lucky. Footnote: still questionable even from beyond the grave, the WHA made headlines in '95 when it "name" will shift the spotlight from "Are you supposed to be here?" to "I'm mortified by my lack of global savvy." Eavesdrop to build a small-talk arsenal. For instance, if you've just overheard a middle manager gripe about "Old Man Johnson busting my hump," you now have something to say to pretty much anyone at the breakfast – except Old Man Johnson. Don't be afraid to go back for seconds or linger over coffee. (As an "employee," you've earned this special time.) If detection appears imminent, act flustered: "I've just been transferred from Toronto and your strange customs scare me."

Finally, should a chase ensue, take comfort in the likelihood that your pursuer is half-drunk.

was revealed that several former players had yet to cash in their pensions – a princely sum rumoured to be in the high three digits.

Soccer

He may have wooed the Flames away from Atlanta, but Nelson Skalbania's golden touch was short-lived, and his Calgary Boomers (North American Soccer League) proved a too-tough sell for Cowtown. Although not a NelSkal project, the Canadian Soccer League's Calgary Kickers went belly-up in '87, despite on-field triumph. Footnote: the team's owner's 62 year-old father (a blind diabetic) threatened a hunger strike if the city didn't cool its soccer apathy. Hunger strike?! That's *soooo* '80s.

Roller Hockey

The timelessly-named Calgary Rad'z folded in '95 after two money-sucking seasons. Owner Larry Ryckman said the sport hadn't caught fire in Canada the way it had in the States. Just you wait.

Secret Views

Photo: Kaya Wiggens

Scotchman's Hill isn't a secret (just ask any bleary-eyed Ramsay resident during Stampede), but it really is a great vantage point for fireworks and/or chuck-wagon action. (The hill's controversial name refers to the stereotype about Scottish people really liking fireworks.)

Those wishing to avoid the Hill's nightly crush of bodies should befriend someone living at Rocky Mountain Court (221-6th Ave. SW). It may seem far away from the Stampede grounds, but the apartment's southside tenants have a great balcony view of not only fireworks, but the U.S. Embassy. (Nice flagpole, Uncle Sam.) All that, and within walking distance of the refrigerator.

If you can't weasel into Rocky Mountain Court, hike into the Reader Rock Garden (SE corner of the Macleod Trail/25th Ave. intersection). The late William Reader spent 29 years as Calgary's parks superintendent, during which time he introduced many non-indigenous plants into his rock garden. More importantly, the roof of the groundskeeping shed affords a great freebie shot of the chucks. Sadly, neighbouring trees are endangering this skinflint's paradise. (Viva la clearcut!)

Good fences may in fact make good neighbours, but they sure wreak havoc on the ol' pocketbook. Ten bucks just to get *into* the Stampede?! Yeah, there's always that lone "free admission before 9 a.m." morning (unofficially extended 'til 9:30 by peace-loving box-office clerks not wishing to incite a riot), but what does a corndog-loving cheapskate do during the rest of the week? (That is, other than sleep overnight behind the Coca-Cola Stage.) Maybe you can sweet-talk your way in through the "out" door ("My dog licked off my re-admission handstamp"), but a better bet is to slip onto the bike path (south of the Stampede grounds and north of the Elbow, just off Macleod Trail) and scout around for a hole in the fence. Don't ask me why, but there's *always* a hole in the fence. You're on your own from there.

Disclaimer: I'm not advocating sneaking into the Stampede through said hole, nor am I suggesting that midway carnies are solely interested in their next smoke break and are therefore disinclined to bust trespassers. Nope, I'm not suggesting nuthin'.

Photo: Sven Schwinn

Bownessie

I swear I once read about a "sea monster" which inhabited the Bowness Park lagoon circa 1900. The terrified locals eventually banded together to kill the monster then roasted it over a fire-pit as some sort of perverted celebration. It couldn't have tasted very great. Anyway, do you think I could find the darn article? Nope. You'll just have to trust me. Besides, people have unearthed prehistoric elephant skeletons in Bowness, so a lagoon monster's not that big of a stretch. Shameless, semi-related plug: they don't serve barbecued sea serpent, but Bowness Park's Lagoon Café & Cappuccino Bar is a charming place nonetheless.

Photo: Blaine Kyllo

Rugby players are fond of saying, "Soccer is a gentlemen's sport played by ruffians. Rugby is a ruffian's sport played by gentlemen." The sport's local history dates back to 1883, when a group of RCMP issued an challenge to any takers willing to play. Today, there are several rugby teams in the city, many with their own clubhouse — none of which are complete without an on-site pub. (At press time, it was unclear who liked the pub part most: the ruffians or the gentlemen?)

The Hornets are the latest Calgary rugby team to inhabit a clubhouse known as "The Bunker" (5721-1A St. SW), so-called because it's basically just a door leading into a basement. The upper floors fell victim to fire and money (a lack of the latter, too much of the former), but as long as there's beer inside somewhere. . . . Other city clubhouses:

Calgary Rugby Union
Shepard Rd. SE

Calgary Canucks Rugby Club
416 Park Ave. SW

Calgary Irish Rugby Club
4334-18th St. NE

Saints Rugby Club
3003-15th St. NE

Saracens Rugby Club
4421-21st Ave. NW

John Gilchrist has reviewed restaurants for CBC radio in Calgary since 1980. With almost 1,000 reviews under his belt (literally) he is regarded as Calgary's foremost expert on food. He teaches food and culture programs for the University of Calgary, cooking classes for the Cookbook Co. Cooks, and co-writes a column in *Avenue* magazine with his wife Catherine Caldwell. They have also released the Millennium Edition of *My Favourite Restaurants in Calgary and Banff*, a compilation of over 150 reviews of the best food in the Foothills. On the next few pages he shares his wealth (and weight) of food knowledge to spare you the time, cost, and aggravation of wasting your time and appetite on lesser efforts.

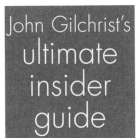

John Gilchrist's
ultimate
insider
guide

Standing on a street corner in an unknown city, pangs of hunger stirring up desires for that favourite café back home, a row of undiscovered restaurants staring back at you. Where to go, what to eat, who to trust? It takes years to get the feel for a city's cuisine, to uncover the hidden gems, to expose the fakers and wannabes. To save you the effort we have asked someone who has put more than 19 years into exploring the food scene in Calgary.

when bad things happen . . .

I hate bad food. Of any kind. At any price. Even free. I love good food. Every meal should be a pleasant experience whether it is a bowl of KD eaten at the kitchen table or a roasted duck breast glazed with a sundried cranberry reduction served in the most elegant surroundings. Any cuisine can be elevated to gourmet status if done right, and dragged into the gutter when combined with inept execution and snotty service.

I hate it when folks come to Calgary – or any other city for that matter – and have lousy food. Every city I have ever been in is capable of both, whether it is Paris or Red Deer. But I recognize the difficulty in searching out the good places, of being able to sort the good from the mediocre. And to find the kind of place that fits your personal style, desire, and appetite.

So I am happy to share a short list of some of my favourites in Calgary. This is a town with a lot of breadth in food – there may not be a lot of depth in certain areas – and excellent value. Prices have started to push upwards of late but I think that you will find great diversity and great prices.

Dine on!

Romantic Rooms

Under the old Love Shoppe sign at Divino (817 - 1st St. SW, 263-5869) or beneath the vines on the patio at Cilantro (338 - 17th Ave. SW, 229-1177) or inside one of the cozy rooms at Mescalero (1315 - 1st St. SW, 266-1133). For those without a Viagra problem, perhaps the Panorama Room atop the Calgary Tower (101 - 9th Ave. SW, 266-7171).

Gone Fishin'

Calgarians have taken to sushi like fish to water, elevating it to preferred power-lunch status. But we like it even better if the nigiri and tekka are delivered by machines rather than people. For the best in auto-delivery climb aboard the sushi train at the Yuzuki (510 - 9th Ave. SW, 261-7701) or trawl the sushi boat bar at the Sakana Grill (116 - 2nd Ave. SW, 290-1118). The fleet is also in at the new Sushi Ginza (Willow Park Village, 10816 Macleod Trail S, 271-9642).

Castle Callebaut

In 1982 a long, lean Belgian named Bernard scoured North America for the perfect location for his burgeoning chocolate empire. He chose a small shop on 17th Avenue SW – now Savoir Fare – and started producing the best chocolates this side of Brussels. Almost two decades later, the Callebaut factory has been moved to a beautiful new building with a walk-through observation centre, and over 40 branch outlets have been opened across Canada and the U.S. For a chance to worship at the shrine and perhaps cadge a free sample, drop by Castle Callebaut at 1313 - 1st St. SE.

BEST ROOMS TO CLOSE A DEAL IN, OR JUST TO GET SOMEONE TO DO SOMETHING THEY DON'T NECESSARILY WANT TO

The heavily wooded Buchanan's (738 - 3rd Ave. SW, 261-4646), the sumptuously Mediterranean Da Paolo (121 - 17th Ave. SW, 228-5556) or the crisp and austere dining room of Teatro (200 - 8th Ave. SW, 290-1012).

BEST BUDGET BUSINESS DINNER

Have a bowl of Vietnamese *bun* at Saigon (1221 - 12th Ave. SW, 228-4200), power up with sushi from the sushi train at the Yuzuki (510 - 9th Ave. SW, 261-7701), or toss back your tie and experience the joy of sausage at Spolumbo's (1308 - 9th Ave. SW, 264-6452).

BEST PRIVATE DINING ROOMS

Groups up to 30 can fit into the newly re-done back room at the Kashmir (507 - 17th Ave. SW, 244-2294) for lovely Northern Indian and Kashmiri cuisine; the Grand Isle in Chinatown (128 - 2nd Ave. SW, 269-7783) can accommodate groups of varying sizes for contemporary Cantonese food in a number of rooms; and Leo Fu has a room that can fit about 25 in the South (511 - 70th Ave. SW, 255-2528). Then there are the semi-private snugs of the James Joyce (114 Stephen Avenue Walk SW, 262-0708), the dimly lit recesses of Mescalero (1315 - 1st St. SW, 266-1133), or you can just rent the entire Big Rock Grill for the gang — up to about 150 (5555 - 76th Ave. SE, 720-3239).

BEST BUSINESS LUNCH

Check out the options in Bankers Hall (315 Stephen Ave. Walk SW) where the suit and tie crowd chow down on the French-Vietnamese delights of Indochine (263-6929) on the Plus-15 level or lounge comfortably on the ground floor in the booths of David Picciotto's The Wine Gallery (290-1091). Outside the downtown core, lunch meetings shape up at the Café Metro (7400 Macleod Trail SW, 255-6537) and in the trendy confines of Simon's (4820 Northland Drive NW, 210-1166).

BEST BRUNCH

Hands down the best brunch with the best view is at the Priddis Greens Golf Course (Priddis area, 931-3171) run by the always charming Bernard Duvette. The highest restaurant in town — the Naturbahn Teahouse (Canada Olympic Park, 247-5465) — comes a close second for the combination of food and view.

BEST PATIOS

The newly re-done Fusion patio is a sunny delight that matches the creative food (514 - 17th Ave. SW, 228-9830), while down the street Cilantro has the benefit of a few years and a higher wall (338 - 17th Ave. SW, 229-1177).

Ginger Beef

Back in the mid-'70s two sisters named Alice and Louise opened the Home Food Inn and the Silver Inn respectively. With identical menus of Beijing (then Peking) cuisine, they became the first in Calgary to offer chicken and cashews in yellow bean sauce, hot and sour soup, and grilled dumplings. Pretty common stuff now, but a quarter century ago it was pretty new. And for a public that grew up on the time-locked Cantonese delights of pineapple chicken balls and sweet and sour pork, pretty adventurous stuff. So they introduced a beef dish that they thought would appeal to the red meat fans. Breaded, deep-fried, and sauced with ginger and chilis, it became known as ginger beef. Now Calgary can lay claim to being the ginger beef capital of the world with dozens of renditions available. To return to the source, try Alice's version at the Bow Restaurant (3406 Bow Trail SW, 686-3799) or Louise's at the Silver Inn (2702 Centre St. N, 276-6711).

Burger à La Français

It can be awfully hard to find a quality burger these days. They are either mass-produced at the typical fast food places or elevated to yuppiedom with certified cuts of rarefied beef, blackberry ketchup, and hand-rolled rolls. Where's a person to get a good old drippy double deluxe cheeseburger? Boogie's (908 Edmonton Trail NE, 230-7070). The burgers are as fresh and well constructed as we could wish and it is worth the trip just to meet the owners. This French couple has run Boogie's since the late '60s but have never really left Paris. Citron pressé with a mushroom burger? Espresso and a twist of lemon with your spicy fries? This is the place.

There is a penchant for opening restaurants in historic buildings, most of which are in the downtown core. But to really experience the past it is worth the short haul to Inglewood for the Deane House (806 - 9th Ave. SE, 269-7747), part of Fort Calgary and named after a commander of the Mounties, and the Cross House (1240 - 8th Ave. SE, 531-2767), the original home of A. E. Cross, one of the Big Four and founder of the Calgary Brewery. Farther downriver at the Bow Valley Ranch in Fish Creek Park (15979 Bow Bottom Trail SE), both the old foreman's house and the ranchhouse itself have been converted into historically accurate but tastefully contemporary restaurants. Annie's (225-3920) and The Ranche (225-3939) rest in a beautiful setting and serve fabulous food.

The two best French restaurants in Calgary come under the direction of a pleasant Moroccan named Mohammed. An accomplished chef himself, he personally oversees the sauteed magret of duck and tarte Tatin at Jo Jo Bistro Parisien (917 - 17th Ave. SW, 245-2382) while Le Grand Saucier himself – Patrice Durandeau – runs the show at Fleur de Sel (2015 - 4th St. SW, 228-9764). To add to the frivolity, Jo Jo's other chef – Hassan – is the identical twin of chef Hussein at the Sultan's Tent next door (909 - 17th Ave. SW, 244-2333). (Actually, we just heard that Hassan has left Jo Jo but we understand that he and Hussein remain twins.)

Virginia's has installed a bank of heaters on their lovely patio (1016 - 8th St. SW, 294-0890) and you can't beat the second floor deck at Break the Fast (516 - 9th Ave. SW, 265-5071) for Stampede Parade watching. For a little taste of history there is the lovely garden patio at The Cross House Garden Café (1240 - 8th Ave. SE, 531-2767) and the freshly-constructed porches of The Ranche in Fish Creek Park (15979 Bow Bottom Trail SE, 225-3939). But the best are still the sultry Southwestern patios of Mescalero (1315 - 1st St. SW, 266-1133) and the terraced – and often poplar-fluffed – patio at the River Café (Prince's Island, 261-7670).

BEST BARS TO MEET DOWNTOWN

The Auburn Saloon with its stunning location in the old Dominion Bank building (712 - 1st St. SE, 266-6628) and the James Joyce with its stunning location in the old Toronto Bank building (114 Stephen Ave. Walk SW, 262-0708). Or, slip under the tracks for a cool one on the deck at Buzzards (1st St. & 10th Ave. SW, 263-7900).

Big Rock

What do you do with a micro-brewery that gets so popular and big that it is no longer a micro-brewery? Move to larger digs, grab one of the best chefs in the city, open a tasty café, and keep brewing great beer. Ed McNally just never quits. He saw the great barley and hops and water available to Albertans and wondered why our beer tasted so bad. But rather than just crying in his beer he did something about it and Big Rock was born. Looks like he wasn't the only one to think that this was a good idea. Check out the new brewery (5555 - 76th Ave. SE) and the fancy Big Rock Grill (720-3239) for food that goes really well with a beer.

BEST BUTCHER

Randy and Gerry are outstandingly friendly for a couple of guys who spend their days cutting up red meat. They are also very good at what they do at The Better Butcher (385 Heritage Dr. SE, 252-7171).

BEST RED MEAT BUZZ

The wonderfully-sauced tenderloins of Fleur de Sel (2015 - 4th St. SW, 245-8187), the steak and kidney pies of the Little Chef (555 Strathcona Blvd. SW, 242-7219), and the big beef bones of Out West (Eau Claire Market, 261-3933).

A Room With a View

One way to test a true Calgarian is to ask what that big tower thing is downtown. If they say it is the Calgary Tower, they are a transplant. If they say it is the Husky Tower, they are pre-Centennial Calgarians and are therefore legitimate. High atop the Tower *(101 - 9th Ave. SW, 266-7171)*, there is a pretty decent restaurant – The Panorama Room – with the world's largest barbecue (the Olympic torch) but no outdoor dining. The restaurant rotates at two different speeds – a 45-minute revolution during lunch and a 60-minute spin at dinner – to create atmosphere and deliver a spectacular view. The food is not bad if you can focus on it instead of what's going on in Bankers Hall. My favourite part is when people put their valuables (purses, briefcases, kids) on the window ledge and then they get left behind while the tables rotate.

BEST BOWL OF NOODLES

The sound of slurping is overpowering local lunch hours as Calgarians indulge in noodly decadence. Some of the best are the subtle Vietnamese *bun* at Trong-Khanh *(1115 Centre St. N, 230-2408)*, the Japanese soba noodles at Cafe de Tokyo *(630 - 1st Ave. NE, 264-2027)*, and the blazing Malaysian creations of the Kuala Lumpur *(132 - 3rd Ave. SE, 265-7998)*. For the painfully hip there is also the multicultural noodle experience of Pongo *(534 - 17th Ave. SW, 209-1073)*.

Photo: Blaine Kyllo

MOST ROMANTIC IF THE RELATIONSHIP IS PROGRESSING SATISFACTORILY

In front of the fireplace on a drizzly night at the River Café *(Prince's Island, 261-7670)* or at one of the window tables at Fusion *(514 - 17th Ave. SW, 228-9830)*.

BEST PANCAKES OUTSIDE OF STAMPEDE SEASON

The Dutch treats of the Pfanntastic Pannenkoek Haus *(2439 - 54th Ave. SW, 243-7757)*

The Tom Yam soup at Thai Sa-On (351-10th Ave. SW, 264-3526), the jerk chicken at Sam's Caribbean One-Stop (3745 Memorial Dr. SE, 248-2113), or anything vindaloo at the Rajdoot (2424 - 4th St. SW, 245-0181). Or just cozy up to a lamb souvlaki and a bottle of ouzo at Santorini Taverna (1502 Centre St. N, 276-8363) and spend the winter.

**BEST RENDITION OF A
NEW YORK RESTAURANT**

Belvedere is the hot place for smart looks, cutting-edge cuisine, and skyscraper prices (107 Stephen Ave. Walk SW, 265-9595) while Florentine (1014 - 8th St. SW, 232-6028) impresses with pomegranate molasses reductions and lovely desserts. Meanwhile, Teatro bounces with sound and flavor on Olympic Plaza (200 Stephen Ave. Walk SE, 290-1012).

BEST VEGETARIAN

Many restaurants have answered the call of the increasing interest in vegetarian cuisine. Some of the best are the Restaurant Indonesia (1604 - 14th St. SW, 244-0645) for the tempeh and gado-gado and the King and I (822 - 11th Ave. SW, 264-7241) for its Thai delights. For the full-tilt veggie hit try Buddha's Veggie (9737 Macleod Trail SW, 252-8830). Everything is vegetarian, even the ginger beef and the salt and pepper eel — made out of mushrooms. Or veg out at the Tuesday night vegetarian buffet at the Rajdoot (2424 - 4th St. SW, 245-0181).

The King Drank Here

Opened as The Grill café and bar in 1914, there are few more historically interesting places in the city than the dining room at the Palliser Hotel (133 - 9th Ave. SE, 262-1234). Renamed The Rimrock in 1962 by Banff artist Charlie Beil, whose rimrock mural adorns the south wall, the room has hosted VIPs from Cary Grant and Juan Antonio Samaranch (not dining together) to Edward VIII when he was still a prince and before he met that nice lady and settled down. Evidently he was very fond of the beverages. With its leather-paneled columns, high, arched windows, and Alberta beef buffet, this is one of the tastiest places to absorb a bit of the old ranch tone of Calgary.

A Slice of the Old West

If you like your tales of the Old West to be more current, check out Buzzards Cowboy Cuisine (1st St. & 10th Ave. SW, 263-7900) during their annual Testicle Festival. Every summer Stuart Allan and his staff serve up "prairie oysters" in various forms. There is the Italian Stallion in a spicy tomato sauce and a version served with gently crushed walnuts. Buzzards guarantees you'll have a ball and if you don't the boss will go nuts. It is worth the visit just to watch international tourists indulge in this rubbery treat.

High-Test

Calgary was a fully-caffeinated burg long before the Seattle folks blew into town. With many offices opening at 7 a.m., Calgarians like to start the day with a jolt from one of these independent coffee purveyors: The Roasterie (314 - 10th St. NW, 270-3304 or 227 - 10th St. NW, 283-8131), Caffe Beano (1613 - 9th St. SW, 229-1232), Joshua Tree (805 Edmonton Trail NE, 230-9228), Blends (1312 Edmonton Trail NE, 230-3226) or our personal favourite, The Planet (2214 - 4th St. SW, 244-3737 and 101 Bowridge Dr. NW, 288-2233).

To Market, to Market

Beyond the bland sameness of the major grocery stores are some smaller and often more interesting options for shopping. Figbelly's *(719 - 17th Ave. SW, 228-7898)* provides ready-to-go meals like sundried tomato risotto and yellowfin tuna with fruit salsa, that need a little re-heating in a millennium spin on the TV dinner. Lina's Italian Market *(2211 Centre St. N, 277-9166)* offers a full-blown Italian market with cheeses and meats and vegetables along with a sparkling Italian café. Need a pie for dessert? Pies Plus *(12445 Lake Fraser Dr. SE, 271-6616)* fills flaky crusts with fresh fruits and real cream fillings that will take the edge off any hunger. The arrival of Debaji's Fresh Market *(5111 Northland Dr. NW, 202-3500)* has taken grocery shopping to a whole new level. With 25,000 square feet of fresh products Debaji's presents a broad range of organics, certified beef, great cheeses, and a lovely café.

A Recipe for Sausage

Take four former Stampeder football players (Mike Palumbo, Craig Watson, and Tom and Tony Spoletini), add in some hearty lineman appetites and Gramma's traditional recipes, and you get Spolumbo's Sausage. With a brand new plant and café at *1308 - 9th Ave. SE (264-6452)*, the boys are pumping out some of the best and most creative sausage around. The sausage is unrepentantly meaty but very innovative with varieties like roasted pepper, pinenut, and turkey along with chicken and apple and dozens of others. Try the meatloaf or meatball sandwiches on-site for the real Spolumbo experience. And I am not just saying that because any one of them could snap me like a twig.

greasy spoons

The greasy spoon of my early youth was Greenan's BA (as in British American Oil) on Highway 2 by the water tower in Wetaskiwin. It was, not surprisingly, done in tones of odd '50s green with a row of green naugahyde booths and green vinyl stools pushed up against a green arborite counter. My dad was a trucker and sometimes I would get to go along on short hauls, trips that would end with a vanilla milkshake and some greasy fries at Greenan's. I later graduated to the Stanley Café — that uniquely prairie hybrid of Chinese and Western Cuisine greasy spoon — for greasy fries and greasy chop suey. So whenever my cholesterol drops I get a craving for the sticky feel of a padded vinyl bench beneath me, a broken jukebox selector on the wall, and a lumpy vanilla milkshake. And, of course, some greasy fries. Here's where I go:

Some restaurants live in obscure locations. Others serve unique or unusual foods or cuisines that are currently out of vogue. Many deserve their obscurity but many are really quite good. They just have not found the way into our culinary psyche. Our picks for the best unsung restaurants in Calgary are as follows. Mimo (4909 - 17th Ave. SE, 235-3377) serves wonderful Portuguese food in an incredibly hard-to-find location: way out 17th Avenue in the Little Saigon mall. Once you find it – in the second row of buildings – you have to go through a very smoky bar, down a long hallway, and into a windowless room at the back. The trip is worth it. The Marathon (130 - 10th St. NW, 283-6796) is in the busy Kensington area but serves little-known Ethiopian food. Service is slow but the opportunity to eat with your hands makes this a tasty stop. Il Girasole (636 - 10th Ave. SW, 263-6661) is one of the best Italian restaurants in the city and is run by Tony Gloria, a top-notch manager. But with the glut of Italian food and its building pushed up against the tracks, it has never received the attention it deserves. The Savoury Café (322 - 11th Ave. SW, 205-4002) boasts a great chef but hides behind the Santa Fe Grill. It is a tiny place but look for it and you will be rewarded with lovely grilled panini and other contemporary delights. Calgary's only South American café is in an out-of-the-way location at 3842 - 19th St. NW. The Blue House features chef Gus Estrada's interpretations of his Colombian food heritage (284-9111). But the obscurity award goes to the Anpurna (175 - 52nd St. NE, 235-6028) for its vegetarian Gujarati cuisine and its behind-the-gas-station address. Gujarat is a province of western India and it produces a cuisine that is light, fresh, spicy, and healthy. Why the Anpurna serves it out of this homely, almost invisible space is beyond us.

MOUNTAIN MECCA CAFE

10231 West Valley Road SW, 286-4891. (Just off Trans-Canada.)

Decor: Two trailers cobbled together; hook and eye latches on the washroom doors.

Standard price: $8 for 3 eggs, bacon, ham, sausage, pancakes, hashbrowns, and toast.

Bottomless coffee: yes

Comments: Great pit stop on the way to the mountains. Can get a bit smoky.

GALAXIE DINER

1413 - 11th St. SW, 228-0001

Decor: Full (and legitimate) retro-diner package. Non-smoking.

Standard price: $5.50 for the Galaxie Burger – loaded with cheese, mushrooms, bacon, peppers, and served with fries.

Bottomless coffee: yes

Comments: Great look, Ford commercials with two grumpy guys shot here. The vinyl is as real as vinyl gets.

get outta town

Calgarians take to the hills at the tiniest opportunity to bike, hike, blade, board, slide, or just eat. We justify our mountain hungers by pointing to the altitude of Banff and our prairie thirsts by acknowledging the dryness of the plains. Wherever we go, good food and drink cannot be far behind. Here's a few places that are hiding in the hills:

La P'tite Table

La Table's contemporary-traditional French food, prepared by a young Paris Hotel School-trained couple, is fabulous. Planted in the old post office in Okotoks (52 North Railway St., 938-2224), it is just a short but tantalizing drive from the city.

Memories Inn

Longview is named that for a reason. There are few better views of the mountains; that is why Clint Eastwood chose this as the key location to shoot *Unforgiven*. His chair hangs on the wall at Memories (558-3665) where they serve the best Western buffet in the area. The ribs and the ambiance are unbeatable.

Le Bistro

More transplanted young French folks run Le Bistro in Canmore, and they do a terrific job on the croque-monsieurs, apple tarts, and almond croissants. Before arriving in Canmore one of the group was a major pastry chef in Montréal where he created Celine Dion's wedding cake. It is startling to see such skill in such a tiny, simple space that looks more like a ski shack than a gourmet café. 718 - 10th St., Canmore, 678-3747.

NELLIE'S
2308 - 4th St. SW, 209-2708
738 - 17th Ave. SW, 244-4616
Decor: Retro-Agrarian. Non-smoking.
Standard price: $8.75 for the Bellybuster — 3 eggs, French toast or pancakes, Bacon, ham, or sausage, toast, and hashbrowns.
Bottomless coffee: yes
Comments: Great service, crowded rooms, rustic feel with uptown style.

BLACKFOOT TRUCK STOP
1840 - 9th Ave. SE, 265-5964
Decor: Real truck stop with real truckers.
Standard price: $6.75 for the Working Man's Breakfast — 2 eggs, hotcake, hashbrowns, toast, and ham, bacon, or sausage.
Bottomless coffee: Need you ask?
Comments: Anatomically correct artwork of 18-Wheelers complete with working lights, and a model train that circles the room.

BREAK THE FAST
516 - 9th Ave. SW, 265-5071
Decor: '70s and '80s album jackets as wall coverings.
Standard price: $8.75 for the breakfast combo — 2 pancakes, 2 eggs, bacon, and homefries.
Bottomless coffee: yes
Comments: Crowded with downtown yuppies but worth the wait.

LION'S DEN

234 - 17th Ave. SW, 265-8482

Decor: Naugahyde booths and stools, Stampede and Flames memorabilia.

Standard price: $5 Clubhouse with fries.

Bottomless coffee: yes.

Comments: Great for pre-Flames pizza or a break from the Stampede grounds.

ROCKIN' ROBIN'S

7007 - 11th St. SE, 252-3067

Decor: Full nouveau-retro package, looks more like a diner than anything from the '50s. Totally non-smoking.

Standard price: $6.25 for the Blow Out Patches (pancakes) and 2 eggs with ham or bacon.

Bottomless coffee: $.50 extra

Comments: This may be the prototype for a new chain but we like it a lot.

The Pines

Banff has often gotten the rap for having bad, expensive food combined with inconsistent service. Much of this has been justified. But with the arrival of The Pines (537 Banff Ave., Rundlestone Lodge, 760-6690) we see a major commitment to excellent contemporary Canadian cuisine, professional service, a lovely room, and reasonable prices – considering the quality.

The Post

Often hyped as "The Great Place" to dine in the Rockies, The Post actually lives up to its reputation. Whether it is a perfect french fry done with a clubhouse sandwich or the roasted veal tenderloin with morel cognac cream sauce and sesame potato gnocchi, The Post delivers in a delightfully lodgy setting.
200 Pipestone Rd., Lake Louise, 522-3989.

The devil goes mountain climbing. Post-secondary graffiti.
Dirty words done dirt cheap. Gonzo granddads and gentlemen
ghostbusters. Fake art and fake identities. Plus: readings, galleries,
and Rudyard Kipling on the joys of . . . Medicine Hat?!

what shall we buy for the drunken sailor?

After speculating on other people's speculations, soldier-turned-lawyer-turned-rancher Eric Harvie (1892-1975) found himself to be a stinkin' rich oil tycoon. The black gold (or, for you hillbillies, "Texas tea") allowed Harvie to indulge his passions for: (a) exotic travel, and (b) buying anything that wasn't nailed down. A reclusive man, he hid behind the Glenbow Foundation, established in 1954 and named for his ranch. Inspired by his pal Norm Luxton (of Banff museum fame), Harvie spent his sizable fortune amassing an amazing collection of, well, *stuff*. Harvie ordered Glenbow Foundation staff "to go out and collect like a bunch of drunken sailors" and collect they did, filling crates with everything from mounted butterflies to Queen Victoria's underwear. (The Foundation eventually split into two divisions: the staff collected artifacts relating to Western Canadian history while Harvie collected whatever he damn well pleased. Methinks the royal panties constituted the latter.) Harvie's collection later became the Glenbow Museum, but only a fraction of his treasures ever see the light of exhibition. This is partially due to space constraints, partially due to the "incorrect" nature of many items. Yep, it's true: there are shrunken human heads hidden in the Glenbow's vaults.

But puckered craniums aren't the drunken sailor's only legacy. Robert Kroetsch's novels *Alibi* and *The Puppeteer* feature Jack Deemer, "a millionaire Calgary oilman whose pastime it was to collect anything that was loose." Sound familiar? Indeed, Kroetsch admits he partially based his eccentric recluse on you-know-who.

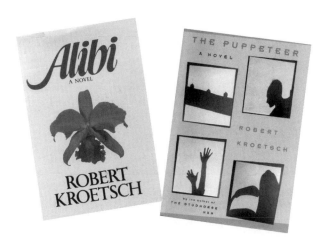

Leon the Frog

You know it's a university 'cuz even the vandalism is wordy. Beginning in the basement and continuing to the roof, the stairwell of the University of Calgary Social Science tower tells the story of Leon the Frog. Nobody knows who wrote it, but the step-by-step tale (with each "chapter" corresponding to whichever faculty occupied that particular floor) has been part of campus lore for years. Legend has it that the author jumped from the roof upon completion. It's doubtful, but who knows. An even stranger rumour is that Leon's story is worth the lung-burstin' effort. That one's definitely false:

Up hop, up hop, hop, up up up, hop, up, hop up, up up up hop, up hop, hop up, up hop up hop. The light at the top of the stairs was not yet visible to Leon as he plopped into the coffee cup of Dr. Mildew Dreary. Unknown to Leon and the [unintelligible] catering company, Leon's mother was a coffee machine. He realized he was a frog and opened his mouth and croaked. "Ribbit." The bleary Dr. Dreary took a gulp of her coffee but not until she reached this stairwell did she cough and realized she had a frog in her throat! She coughed and sputtered and it was the rebirth of Leon. He [unintelligible] around. "Where am I?" said Leon before he could move. [unintelligible] The head of Food Services came down the stairs. "A new sandwich," he said. [unintelligible] [unintelligible] [unintelligible]. . . .

Awww, forget it. Take the elevator.

Got it, Need it, Got it

Zurich artists m. vanci stirnemann and Cat Schick (jeez, isn't anyone named Peter or Paul or Mary anymore?) developed the idea of the "artist trading card," a DIY project designed to break down the traditional art world hierarchy. Make 'em! Swap 'em! Clip 'em to your bike to make motorcycle sounds! It's art *for* the people, *by* the people!

The trading cards are exactly what they sound like: mini (2.5 inches by 3.5 inches) masterpieces created on card stock, except they don't come with a stick of that cruddy pink bubble-gum. Anyone can make 'em, and nobody's gonna rain on your creative vibe: two-dimensional, three-dimensional, thin, chunky . . . everything's cool as long as the finished card slips comfortably into those plastic baseball card collector sleeves.

Calgary artist Chuck Stake imported the trading card idea to the New Gallery (516D-9th Ave. SW, 233-2399), where trading sessions are now held on the last Saturday of the month from 5 to 7 p.m. Swap meets can attract as many as 75 people, ranging in age from kids to seniors, so you just know there's gonna be some hot trading action. Bring your bike.

Ground Zero

Ground Zero's pop culture jones embraces sci-fi nerd nostalgia (Stephen Massicotte's *The Boys' Own Jedi Handbook*) and youth-gone-bad drama (Eric Bogosian's *subUrbia*, Mark Ravenhill's *Shopping & Fucking*).

Sage Theatre

Sage Theatre debuted in '98 with Judith Thompson's *Lion in the Streets*. Subsequent works such as *Slavs!* (Tony Kushner) and *Reading Hebron* (Jason Sherman) confirmed the company's commitment to complicated, uh, stuff.

Theatre in Exile

Theatre in Exile's heady mandate is to present contemporary non-English plays in translation. And that's exactly what they've done with Quebecois works such as Michel Marc Bouchard's *Lilies* and *The Orphan Muses*, plus Carole Frechette's *The Four Lives of Marie*.

Suffragette City

Photo: Glenbow Archives NA 15143

From 1923 to 1935, Nellie McClung lived and wrote at 803-15th Ave. SW. Her opponents thought her a "hyena in petticoats," but there's no denying she rocked the vote like nobody's beeswax. A few blocks away is Nellie's Kitchen (738B-17th Ave. SW) which, ironically enough, has absolutely nothing to do with McClung. But great eggs benedict all the same.

Bob Edwards is the unsung granddaddy of gonzo journalism. After sharpening his teeth on a French Riviera tourist scandal sheet, Edwards unleashed his masterful *Eye Opener* on March 4, 1902. Under the mandate "It is a mistake to spoil a good story by sticking too closely to facts," the erratically-published newspaper mixed accurate reporting with even more accurate lies, making it impossible to distinguish between either. As the *Eye Opener's* founder/publisher/staff, Edwards attacked any target he deemed guilty of "dinky little prejudices."

From his unofficial "office" in the bar of the Alberta Hotel (kitty-corner to the downtown Bay), Edwards lobbied for the creation of Tanglefoot University, where "lectures on Alcoholic Hallucinations will be given once a week by one who has been there, accompanied by colored illustrations of alligators, pink rats, performing elephants." (Off the page, Edwards wrestled with his own alcoholism.) *The Eye Opener* offered the fictional opinions of Bertie Buzzard-Chlomondeley and Peter J. Puddicum, as well as Peter J. McGonigle, editor of the non-existent *Midnapore Gazette*. Contributing to the madness were the straight-up Presbyterian and Methodist church notices which Edwards ran *gratis*. News of Edwards' satiric shenanigans travelled the world, earning him both accolades and lawsuits.

Bob Edwards died in 1922. His wife sealed the final *Eye Opener*, along with his well-used whiskey flask (full, of course), in the base of his Union Cemetery headstone. To find "Eye Opener Bob," walk south from the Macleod Trail pedestrian overpass to section R; his grave is along the fence.

Photo: Glenbow Archives NA 450-1

Literary Readings

Just like books-on-tape, but harder to take with you in the car.

Ex Libris
A co-presentation of the Calgary Public Library & Pages On Kensington, Ex Libris brings in big names like Douglas Coupland and P.J. O'Rourke.

Photo: Blaine Kyllo

Java Sharks
529-17th Ave. SW, 244-5552
Open mic poetry every Sunday at 8 pm. Big turnout, so get there early to sign up.

Markin-Flanagan Distinguished Writers Program
Based at the U of C, and funded by a pair of lit-lovin' tycoons, the Markin-Flanagan program sponsors both a Canadian writer-in-residence and visits by international writers.

Photo: Glenbow Archives NA 177-1

Born of mixed heritage in 1890, Sylvester Long picked up a handful of Cherokee words from a visiting Wild West show and began passing himself off as "Long Lance," a full-blooded Native. He left his North Carolina home for the Carlisle Indian School in Pennsylvania, and later bluffed his way into West Point. (Fearing detection, he skipped off for the less-picky Canadian army, and fought at Vimy Ridge with Princess Patricia's Canadian Light Infantry.)

Long Lance landed a post-war reporting gig for the *Calgary Herald*, where he made a name for himself writing about the Plains Indians. On a less literary note, he garnered national attention for lobbing a fake bomb into City Hall. (Actually, he pulled the ol' bowling-ball-with-lit-fuse stunt on several occasions. Long Lance would stage the prank while disguised with a mask, then dutifully report it as "news.")

Somewhere along the way Sly started calling himself "Chief Buffalo Child Long Lance of the Blackfoot." The fabrication didn't sit so well with legit Blackfoots, but the gifted charmer (and legendary ladies' man) got away with it. Long Lance's journalistic success took him to New York, where a *Cosmo* editor suggested the fascinating "chief" record his life story. Returning to a Calgary rooming house, Long Lance banged out his "autobiography," liberally cribbed from a friend's real-life Blackfoot childhood.

The Autobiography of Chief Buffalo Child Long Lance (1928) blew through its initial printing of 10,000 copies to became a bestseller. Long Lance parlayed his celebrity into a starring role in Hollywood's "all-Indian" *The Silent Enemy*, a career move which would prove tragic: a co-star discovered his deception and the jig, as they say, was up.

Today it's called "resumé padding," but back then it was baldfaced lying. A disgraced Sylvester Long committed suicide on March 21, 1932, while staying at a millionaire gal-pal's California mansion. (Millionaire? Mansion? California? Talk about bottoming out.) Working the dramatic metaphor 'til the very end, he shot himself in the heart.

Calgary is renowned for its abundance of street art. If nothing else, the various murals/paintings/installations provoke reactions from passersby, which is no small feat. I once watched a punk spend twenty-five minutes balancing a cigarette in the mouth of one of those pear-shaped office-schlubs near the downtown Bay ("Conversation," William McElcheran). And then another half-hour watching kids try to mount Harry O'Hanlon's "Family of Horses" on the Municipal Building steps. Another example: more people are freaked out by the SeaMonkey-ish loafers on 4th St. and 21st Ave. SW ("Hanging Out," Peter Smith) than by any derelict occupying a similar bench. And who can forget the tall, naked people ("Brotherhood of Mankind," Mario Armengol) in front of the Calgary Board of Education? (The freaky nudes used to grace CBE-issue scribblers & notebooks, tempting many underachieving doodlers to give 'em graphite-enhanced willies.)

But the award for weirdest public art goes to . . . the vomiting swan! The old lobby of the CIBC Building *(309-8th Ave. SW)* is decorated with the most bizarre floor-tile mosaic: a grey swan regurgitating food into the awaiting mouths of baby birds. Underneath, the tiles spell "Canada Life Assurance Company." Above, for whatever reason, is a beaver. (For those of you who just can't get enough, the swan/vomit motif is repeated overtop the doorway outside.) And you thought those plastic "drinking birds" were cool.

Young Flesh! Live on Stage!

The theatrical old guard aren't the only show in town anymore. New (and newish) thespians on the block include:

**Back Pocket
Performance Theatre**
Acting! Dancing! Jumping! (Perhaps better known as inter-disciplinary theatre.)

**Mind The Walrus
Theatre Group**
In a word: comedy.

Chimaera Productions
Dedicated to presenting female-centred works like *Steel Magnolias*.

The Shakespeare Company
Go on, take a guess.

**Under The Cover
Theatre Company**
A student group which pops up every now and again with something along the lines of a Mamet play.

**Downright Canadian
Theatre Company**
It's hard to figure out from the name, but the DCTC stages a mixture of new and traditional Canuck plays.

Kipling to World: Don't Hate the Hat

AHEAD BY A CENTURY

In 1982, three Henry Wise Wood students received ten-day suspensions for writing slanderous school newspaper articles. The punishment undoubtedly came with the patented "You'll never amount to anything if you keep this up, young man" speech. Let's check in with the trio and see what became of the scalawags:

One of the delinquents went on to date Moon Unit Zappa and write the Aerosmith episode of *The Simpsons* (not necessarily in that order), so he's doing A-OK. Another is a UK entertainment lawyer — not too shabby. And the third ne'er-do-well is Douglas Century, the self-styled "nice Jewish boy" author of *Street Kingdom: Five Years Inside the Franklin Avenue Posse*, a celebrated undercover account of New York gangsta culture.

Nice work, boys. Unfortunately, there's still the matter of that blemish on your permanent records. A month of detentions all around.

Kevin Bacon is passé — the latest party-game rage is "Six Degrees of Medicine Hat." Wanna play? I knew you would.

We'll start with India's Khajuraho temples, famed for their sizzling erotic sculptures. Continuing the fine tradition of subversion in animation, the saucy structures were the inspiration for the temples in Disney's *The Jungle Book*. *The Jungle Book* was written by Rudyard Kipling. Rudyard Kipling visited Calgary in 1907 as part of a whirlwind Canadian tour; he was so taken with "the wonder city of Canada" that his train was delayed two hours until he finished sightseeing. But Kip's heart belonged to another Albertan wonder, "a wooden town shut in among low, treeless, rolling ground, a calling river that ran unseen between scarped banks . . . a painfully formal public garden with pebble paths and foot-high fir trees . . . some Indians in red blanketing with buffalo horns for sale trailing along the platform, and, not ten yards from the track, a cinnamon bear and a young grizzly standing up with extended arms in their pens and begging for food. . . . The only commonplace thing about the spot was its name — Medicine Hat, which struck me instantly as the only possible name such a town could carry."

There you go: six degrees of Medicine Hat!

Actually, Kipling's love of the Hat was more than a passing fling. A few years later, when he got wind that Medicine Hat was considering a civic namechange due to constant ribbing from the *Calgary Herald*, Rudy weighed in with a heartfelt letter. In his missive, later published worldwide (!) as a booklet, he wrote: "I always knew that Calgary called Medicine Hat names, but I did not realize that Medicine Hat wanted to be Calgary's little god-child." After making fun of various American towns (Schenectady, Podunk, Schoharie, Poughkeepsie), Kipling urged Medicine Hat to hang tough.

"What then should a city be re-christened that has sold its name?" he asked, always the drama king. "Judasville."

"Hello Calgary! You're the best hometown I know!" So went a certain TV station's damnably catchy jingle, mercifully since retired. (It was enough to make you turn off the tube and, y'know, go outside or something. Well, almost.) But the Sandstone City has inspired more than just "I-heart-Calgary" boosterism. What follows are some of the city's more — how you say? — *diverse* literary depictions.

Louis de Bernières

In spring '96, British magic-realist Louis de Bernières (*Captain Corelli's Mandolin*, *The Troublesome Offspring of Cardinal Guzman*, etc.) landed in Calgary for a month-long residency with the Markin-Flanagan distinguished writers programme. Two years later, he published the love poem "A Mad British Pervert Has a Sexual Fantasy About the 10th St. Bridge in Calgary" in *Alberta Views* magazine. (Me, I'll take the Crowchild-Glenmore flyover any day. Now that's a hot piece of overpass.) Here's what Louis de B. had to say about his bridge *d'amour*:

Let me speak in praise of the 10th St. Bridge, for she is the shy girl, but

pretty, whom people forget to ask to parties. . . . She is named

Louise, she is prone to sulks, she is suspicious of flattery, she is easily hurt

by teasing, she is wary of boys and confiding with girls, she doesn't wear

make-up because she has puritanical leanings. . . .

Graham Greene

Most people don't associate the Havana Man with the Rocky Mountains, but Graham Greene toured extensively in Western Canada during the 1950s. (Greene's horse-crazy daughter loved the wilderness, and he found Canada to be a pleasant stopover en route to Jamaica.) In Greene's epistolary "Dear Dr. Falkenheim" (1963, found in *Collected Stories*), a distraught father confesses the source of his son's psychological trauma. In what could be safely termed the worstest Christmas ever, the child witnesses a department store promotion go horribly awry, resulting in a rent-a-Santa's grisly decapitation by helicopter.

ONE OF THESE ABSTRACT SCULPTURES DOESN'T BELONG, ONE OF THESE ABSTRACT SCULPTURES JUST ISN'T THE SAME

Engineering students do the darndest things. Back in the '60s, fine arts students installed four abstract sculptures on the west side of the U of C Library Tower. Today there are five. Utilizing their extensive knowledge of mathematics and physics, the 'geers sneaked a fifth sculpture into the mix as one of those "anyone can make modern art" protests. The frightening thing is, it's hard to tell which sculpture is the fake.

A MAN FOR BOWNESS

Back in the '70s, neighbours knew writer/poet/conservationist Sid Marty as that bearded guy who liked to watch kids cannonball off the Bow River train bridge. But the good times couldn't last forever: the *Leaning On The Wind* author traded 6936 Bow Crescent NW for a "ranchette" near Pincher Creek, and CP wrapped the bridge in barbed wire.

The real St. Nick is entombed in Italy, but Greene's fictional bloodbath is set on far more familiar turf:

With my wife and son I had left England for Canada only a few months before and we were none of us yet accustomed to the great steely neon-lit city which lay on the foothills of the Rockies more than three thousand feet up. The sky seemed higher and larger than our English skies, above the level of the clouds we knew, and the air was cold and fresh like lake water. From our bungalow which was called Kosy Nuick on the outskirts of the city we could see across the rolling beige ranchland to the snowy peaks of the Rockies. . . .

We have never returned, so what my son now remembers of the place must be the real memories of a six-year-old. They are an odd assortment when he speaks of them: men dressed like cowboys buying Weetabix in the self-help stores . . . the roar and stamp of a multitude of beasts in the cattle trucks at the station, the arch of cloud above the Rockies which heralded what they call the chinook, when the temperature suddenly rises in a matter of hours from twenty degrees below zero to thirty-five above. . . .

Peter Stinson

Peter Stinson's ellipsis-heavy short story "Taxi" (anthologized in *Concrete Forest: The New Fiction of Urban Canada*) is a gritty slice-of-night-life, an after-hours tour of Calgary's underbelly. (Surprise, surprise: Stinson used to drive a hack in town.) Gee whiz, it's about time Ducky's Pub *(5, 2100-4th St. SW, don't miss karaoke night)* received the CanLit stamp of recognition:

In Kensington, I think some guy's flaggin me but he's not . . . I drive away pissed off but get flagged by a young guy with bleached white hair and piercings . . . goes downtown. . . .

From a downtown hair place, a very attractive woman with strong, pleasant perfume goes to Ducky's Pub. . . .

From Goliath's to Renfrew, a man named Richard, Stonewall T-shirt, so drunk he can hardly walk . . . I help him to the door . . . great garden. . . .

LOCAL BOY SPAWNS DEMON, MAKES GOOD

Todd McFarlane left Calgary to draw Spiderman for Marvel Comics. Then he quit Marvel to create the hellish *Spawn* comic books — a gutsy move which paid off with a movie, HBO cartoon series, creepy toys, and over $75M in his bank account. McFarlane can now afford to live in Phoenix year-round and buy Mark McGwire homerun baseballs, which isn't to say he doesn't have problems. His mom, for example, wouldn't let him buy the Edmonton Oilers. (The reason? Too much money.) Always the rebel multi-millionaire, he did it anyway.

Ken Mitchell

Pig-farmer-turned-novelist Ken Mitchell's 1972 debut, *Wandering Rafferty*, concerns a travelling salesman/rapscallion named Tom Rafferty. At one point in this Rabelaisan (well, so sez the dust-jacket) romp thru the Western provinces, Rafferty moves into "the small and regrettably declining slum area around Ninth Avenue" and begins shilling subscriptions to *Mother Goose* (!) magazine:

Calgary was a moderately attractive city from Rafferty's point of view. There was plenty of money in town - an endless supply of it, by almost anyone's calculations. There proved to be no difficulty at all selling Mother Goose, and there was a good selection of drinking places. After his regular two-hour stint in the suburbs, Rafferty would visit the library and the liquor store, in that order. . . .

From the liquor store, he would drive east toward the park on St. George's Island, calculating to arrive about four o'clock as the afternoon began to cool. There, in the shadow of the towering statues of the dinosaurs which had once roamed the Rocky Mountain foothills, Rafferty spent the summer reading. Everybody else was going wild about Trudeau, the new Liberal party leader, but Rafferty drank wine and watched the girls who came to the park in bikinis to play with their coloured beach balls on the grass.

Katherine Govier

In Katherine Govier's *Between Men* (1987), Calgarians cling to "a few tenets: the mountains were beautiful, and business was good . . . a handshake meant a deal, and art without a horse in it was pretentious." Govier's university instructor protagonist knows that "until you'd lived through a bust and lost your money and started again, you wouldn't belong," but she can't help but question the shiny New West:

Ace sat behind the wheel of his low car, chafing in the glare of the late spring sun. A crane had wheeled into the eastbound lane of the Crowchild Trail in front of him and the procession of cars was caught in its slow wake. Trucks and heavy equipment surrounded them. A new subdivison was going up; the whole hillside was under construction.

"Everything's always going up in this place, nothing's ever finished. Nothing ever gets old." So said Suzanne disconsolately. "Ace? Don't you think? Am I the only person in Calgary who likes things old?"

Fred Stenson

In *Last One Home* (1988), a University of Calgary student named Gabriel learns many things, including the sad truth that the engineering building ("a mad monastery where the monks all wanted miserably to fail at chastity") isn't babe central. In the following scene, Fred Stenson pays homage to that dubious institution, the *Calgary Sun* Sunshine Girl:

On Blackfoot Trail the next morning, in a coffee shop linked to a silent twelve-lane bowling alley. An acre of red arborite surrounded by wooden signs. Messages burned in the wood and varnished over. . . .

Gabriel sat under a wagon wheel chandelier and sipped coffee. Beyond his egg-sticky plate, the morning tabloid lay open, his eyes pointing but not focussing there. It was only when the waitress came to pour more coffee that he realized he had been staring at today's Big Sky Woman. Eyebrow-length bangs cut straight across, face like a bruise. She had on a black halter top with fringes and, beneath that, a deep crease in her midriff as if the top of her body had been given a full turn.

Karen Connelly

St. George killed a dragon and didn't get jack-squat. All Karen Connelly did was *touch* the dragon and she won a Governor General's Award. It's a weird world, no? Anyway, Connelly's teenage Thailand diary could've been subtitled "Escape from Boring Ol' Cowtown," so it's surprising that her 1995 follow-up, *One Room in a Castle*, has some bonafide hometown content. Granted, it's mostly Connelly sitting around in her skivvies and/or drinking, but hey, whatever gets ya thru the night. Happily, the following passage has elements of both grand themes:

I sit on the roof in my underwear.

From here, I see the nearby shining angles of downtown, a brick high school in a green field, old row houses, the busy traffic of Seventeenth Avenue. (Seventeenth Avenue, where I buy wine, bagels, books; where, under the cover of night, I leave empty beer bottles for the raggedy men.)

W.O. Mitchell

W.O. Mitchell's *The Vanishing Point* (1973) tells the story of a good-hearted school teacher working on the Stony Indian Reserve. When his favourite student disappears, Carlyle Sinclair sets off on a rescue mission into a unnamed-yet-familiar "city of half a million people." Only W.O. could, er, *shaft* the Calgary Tower with such precision:

He made the right turn onto Johnston Trail, and they began the shallow descent into the city's heart. Far ahead, the Devonian Tower thrust with stiff arrogance fully a third higher than the tallest of the office buildings around; from the broad cylindrical base the concave slope sides soared six hundred feet, so that its glass revolving restaurant, boutiques, gift shop, broadcasting station, CSFA, floated above traffic smog. Pretty nearly the only six-hundred-foot concrete erection in the British Commonwealth. With a May basket balanced on its tip – that twinkled with colored lights at night. . . . And had a red oil derrick to spear the last fifty feet.

Aritha van Herk

In *Restlessness*, Aritha van Herk's fifth novel, a suicidal women checks into the Palliser Hotel with an ex-Quaker assassin. He gets paid, she gets killed, and everything's jake. At least that's the plan. (When did assisted assassinations become so *complicated*, anyway?) The book is loaded with local landmarks, but the outrageous absence of panhandlers brands the following passage as fiction:

The underpass sidewalk slants upward, and we climb, coming out from beneath the track to the slightly tawdry reach of First Street, the Bible House, Rideau Music, Cedar's Deli, the TransAlta building, the refurbished block of Manhattan Lofts, the IODE shop and at the end of the street, Maxwell Bates' St. Mary's, the cathedral outlined in stark rare form. . . . He gestures at the illuminated spire. "It's a stunning building, beautiful spires."

Who: Ken McGoogan, novelist

LCD: There's lots of Beat-styled substance abuse in McGoogan's two Kerouac-inspired novels (*Visions of Kerouac* and its rewrite, *Kerouac's Ghost*), but the real hot sauce is in *Calypso Warrior*, his steamy novel about sexual indiscretion and, errr, Québec language laws.

Sample: *David put his hands on her shoulders. She turned and came into his arms. Together they fell onto the bed. . . . Now Isabelle Garneau, brilliant Québécoise novelist, lay beneath him with her legs spread, moaning his name. David went wild.*

Who: Rajinderpal S. Pal, poet

LCD: Pal's first collection, *pappaji wrote poetry in a language i cannot read*, tackles cultural heritage, dead dads, and lost languages — not a lot of room for sex, but it's in there. (Bonus marks for namedropping the Ship & Anchor.)

Sample: *foreskin forewarned / for skin hard to the touch / touch then smell your hand . . . trace shapes and words / on backs.*

Henry Rollins

Get In The Van is the '80s tour diary of L.A. punk-rock godfather Henry Rollins. His is a grim world of tattoos, cramped back-seats, bodily odours, headaches, and breakfasts at Denny's. (Whaddaya expect from a muscle-bound grump who writes angst-in-yer-pants poetry with titles like *Now Watch Him Die* and *Pissing in the Gene Pool*?) Here's how Happy Hank described Black Flag's August '85 gig in Calgary:

Pouring rain upon arrival. Davo pulls out the loading ramp and slices his thumb from top to bottom, right to the bone. He looks at it. I look at it. . . . Next, a person pours beer into the tape deck . . . destroyed for good. We do the show. The promoter will not pay us what he promised. He owes us from the last time we were in these parts. He's sitting there - grinning, drinking beers and telling us how he'll pay us in September and how hopefully the check won't bounce. . . .

So we're stuck in Canada for the next while. I don't like it here. None of us do. We pulled into a Denny's this morning to eat.

Not to knock cow-patty paperweights or *découpage*, but there's some stellar non-cowboy artstuff coming out of the city. Ladies & gentlemen, snapshots of three local *artistes* (and one ex-pat) with shiny international reps:

Doug Fraser

He may be a born-and-raised Lethbridge boy, but Doug Fraser lives in Calgary and he's Alberta College of Art and Design alumnus, so that's close enough to call him "son." Simply put, Fraser's illustrations are *everywhere*. He's appeared in pretty much any magazine you can name (a sampling: *Esquire, GQ, Mother Jones, Newsweek, Sports Illustrated* – plus numerous *Time* covers), and has done work for everyone from Sony to the Oakland A's. When in Chicago, be sure to have your picture snapped in front of Fraser's NikeTown mural.

Marianna Gartner

Image: Courtesy of the artist

Marianna Gartner's circus freak paintings feature legless acrobats, elastic-skinned men, dwarf clowns, and the ever-popular half-man/half-woman. (Not to give you the wrong impression, she also paints babies, bugs, and bones.) Her work's been shown internationally, including New York's Forum Gallery and Toronto's Sable-Castelli, and can be seen locally inside the dome of the downtown Alberta Treasury Branch. Celebrity client: Lee Grant, Oscar-winning star of *Shampoo* and *Airport '77*, and proud owner of Gartner's "Waiting for the Devil" parts one & two.

SPECIAL BONUS: GRATUITOUS VIOLENCE!

Who: Sharon Pollock, playwright

LCD: People love historical killings, and Pollock goes for the gold with *Saucy Jack* (as in ". . . the Ripper") and *Blood Relations* (about Lizzie "Forty Whacks" Borden).

Sample: *She approaches her father with the hatchet behind her back. She stops humming. A pause, then she slowly raises the hatchet very high to strike him. Just as the hatchet is about to start its descent, there is a blackout.* (from *Blood Relations*)

THE DEVIL MADE HIM SAY IT

Aleister Crowley was whatcha call a real Renaissance man: writer, tantric sex maniac, self-confessed "drug fiend," practitioner of black magic, and — believe it or not — mountain climber *par excellence*. Yep, the so-called "wickedest man alive" fancied himself a regular Sir Edmund Hillary. (Crowley also claimed to be able to summon the Loch Ness Monster at will — is it any wonder Led Zep axeman Jimmy Page feverishly collected Uncle Al's old ceremonial robes?) Guess that's why Crowley felt qualified to pass judgment on the Rocky Mountains after touring Canada in 1906. "I was very disappointed with the Rockies," he wrote in his autobiography. "They are singularly shapeless; and their proportions are unpleasing. There is too much colourless and brutal base; too little snowy shapely summit." (What, not enough opium orgies in Banff for ya?) Crowley was equally unimpressed with Calgary and its "crude and offensive" citizens who "seem to resent the existence of civilized men." Crude? Offensive?!? Oh yeah? Yer satanic majesty wears cloven-hoofed army boots. So there.

Tom Bagley

With visions of sugarplums and blood-crazed zombies dancing in his head, Tom Bagley has inked a hearse-load of album and T-shirt artwork for the cream of North American garage rock (including Huevos Rancheros, Man . . . Or Astroman?, and his own ghoulish Forbidden Dimension), as well as illustrations for *Ralph*, the *Calgary Straight*, and *VOX*. In 1996, he put the "fine" in fine art with "Nocturnal Eye," an exhibit of 13 glow-in-the-dark screen-prints at the Truck Gallery.

Image: Courtesy of the artist

Attila Richard Lukacs

Edmonton, Vancouver, Berlin: lots of cities lay claim to Attila (a testament to the mom 'n' pop appeal of homo-erotic skinhead paintings), but Calgary supplied the backdrop to the *enfant terrible*'s wonder years. How's this for local cred: Lukacs was fired from his window-dressing job at the downtown Bay. (Use your imagination.) It is reported that Madonna owns at least one original Lukacs painting. Given the Material Girl's reputation for shameless subcultural appropriation, can an Attila-inspired reinvention (shaved head, Doc Martens, oily handprint on bare ass) be far away?

Elementary, My Dear Ectoplasm

When Sir Arthur Conan Doyle, the celebrated creator of Sherlock Holmes, visited Calgary, it wasn't to discuss deerstalker caps and killer dogs. Nope, the topic of Doyle's address to the Al Azhar Temple was fairies and ghosts. (Attendance was poor; Doyle blamed evil supernatural forces.)

Some backstory for ya: the writer's longstanding interest in spiritualism took on greater weight when his brother and son died within weeks of each other. Doyle's self-styled "psychic quest" drew him into a world of automatic trance-writing and communication with the dead. "Why should we fear our dear one's death," he wrote, "if we can be so near to them afterwards?" Years of research – during which time he wrote many books on the subject and claimed to have grasped materialized spirit hands, witnessed objects levitate, and whiffed "the peculiar ozone-like smell of ectoplasm" – convinced Doyle that "the physical basis of all psychic belief is that the soul is a complete duplication of the body, resembling it in the smallest particle, although constructed in some far more tenuous material."

It was in this spirit (pardon the pun) that Doyle made several trips to North America in the early 1900s. One such trip brought him to Calgary, where he lectured on the proper handling of ectoplasm (my guess would be to wear gardening gloves) and warned naysayers against dismissing "spirit photographs." The latter referred to alleged photos of garden fairies, snapped by two British girls. You'd have to be blind to not see thru the cheap deception but Doyle very vocally defended the pics – right up until the moment the girls admitted their forgery. Still, Doyle maintained his faith. (Methinks Sherlock Holmes would've paddled their lyin' behinds and sent 'em to bed without any pixie dust.)

Photo: Courtesy of the Toronto Reference Library

HELL NO, I'M NOT JEAN DOE

Calgary ex-pat Warren Kinsella has worn many hats, including that of Jean Chretien's speechwriter. What Chretien may not realize, however, is Kinsella spent his youth belting out feelgood anthems such as "I am a Confused Teenager" and "The Secret of Immortality." Yep, Kinsella was the bass-playin' mastermind behind local punks the Hot Nasties. (Reminder: if you don't have a copy of the Nasties' 1980 *Invasion of the Tribbles* EP, you just ain't living.)

But punk-rock may not be the lad's only dirty secret. Now a lawyer and author of *Web of Hate: The Far Right Network in Canada*, Kinsella is widely rumoured to be "Jean Doe," the pseudonymous muckraker behind *Party Favours*. (Written with insider insight, *Party Favours* is a thinly-veiled novel about the Chretien government, basically a "*Primary Colors* Goes to Ottawa" sorta thing.)

In 1997, crack journos at the *Hamilton Spectator* devised a clever plan to unmask the anonymous scribbler. While the shadowy author was occupied with an online interview, the sleuths telephoned the top suspects. (The idea being that Doe couldn't surf the 'Net *and* answer his/her phone at the same time. Guess the junior Woodwards & Bernsteins hadn't considered space-age technology like, say, *two phone lines*.) Some of the potential Jean Does, such as *The Globe & Mail's* Susan Delacourt and *Frank's* Michael Bate, were scratched from the list. Other prime suspects weren't so lucky, thanks to busy signals, voice-mail, and other suspicious signs.

As for Kinsella, the hot 'n' nasty one had disappeared without a trace. Sorta. Well, not really. In fact he hadn't disappeared at all — but he *had* just quit his job. (Gimme a break, I'm trying to build some *atmosphere* here.) Does Warren Kinsella = Jean Doe? The mystery continues.

ADIOS, KEMOSABE

Long before he got shoeless with Evelyn Lau, W.P. Kinsella taught "bonehead" English at "Desolate U." (Whoa! That's the *University of Desolation* to you, pal.) After four years and ten months (but who's counting?) in Calgary's "plastic" confines, and with his literary star on the rise, W.P. decamped to the beachfront climes of White Rock, B.C.

No, Not the Guy Who Wrote *Roots*

From sex to weight-loss, Calgary has played a key role in the life of mega-bestselling novelist Arthur Hailey (*Hotel, Airport, Wheels,* and other mono-titles). Today, there are over 160 million copies of his eleven novels in print, but in 1942 he was just another undereducated British kid. Hailey was shipped to Calgary as part of the Commonwealth Air Training Scheme (that's what he calls it: a "scheme"), where he learned to fly twin-engine Airspeed Oxfords at the airport. Rather, he *would have* learned to fly except he contracted the mumps. This didn't affect his luck with the ladies, however, and Hailey fondly recalls losing his virginity under a tree on a grassy slope. He returned to Calgary in 1997 to check whether the slope and/or tree were still there. (Seriously.) They weren't. For all you diehard Hailey fans itchin' for a field trip, the randy septuagenarian reckons the historical spot to be somewhere between 6th & 10th Streets and 34th & 38th Avenues SW. (There's no plaque or marker, just fancy Elbow Park digs.)

As for the weight-loss. . . . In 1962, a *Calgary Herald* reporter interviewed Hailey, who was well on his way to becoming Mr. Bigshot Writer. Hailey credits the resulting article, in which he was referred to as "portly," with kickstarting his lifelong health regime. (Honestly, I'm not making this stuff up.)

Yep, Arthur Hailey holds Calgary dear. But not *that* dear. By 1970 he was making some serious coin, so he bid adieu to Canada's draconian income tax laws and skipped to the free 'n' easy Bahamas. Sigh. At least we'll always have wherever that grassy slope used to be.

Keith Johnstone invented Theatresports as a University of Calgary classroom exercise in 1977; today it's played the world over, and is ranked with Chicago's Second City as a seminal comedy training ground. Johnstone's creation wasn't long for academia, and it soon relocated to the Loose Moose Theatre Company and yadda-yadda-yadda. (Consult Kathleen Foreman and Clem Martini's *Something Like A Drug: An Unauthorized Oral History of Theatresports* for the whole story.) The Theatresports premise is a sort of a wrestling-meets-improv thing: two teams battle for control of the stage by trying to be the most entertaining. There are numerous events, each with a self-explanatory name: "One Word At A Time," "Speaking In One Voice," and the one where the stage action revolves around actors trying to plausibly steal each other's hats. (I think it's called "The Hat Game." Or maybe just "Hat.") Of course, no mention of Theatresports is complete without namedropping its most famous Calgary alumni: ex-Kids in the Hall Bruce McCulloch and Mark McKinney. Loose Moose may have abandoned its NE industrial park home for the artier Garry Theatre in Inglewood, but it still stages Theatresports every Sunday night at 7 p.m.

outdoor festivals

Afrikadey

When: August

What: Weeklong celebration of African culture, featuring drum/dance workshops, music, film, and art exhibitions. Everything wraps up with a big party on Prince's Island.

Calgary Folk Music Festival

When: July

What: A four-day weekend of music, food, and probably mud. Big names on the mainstage, workshops/jams on the smaller stages. Always an eclectic lineup that's far more global than the traditional idea of "folk music." (That said, the FolkFest *did* manage to lure Joan Baez in '99.)

Calgary Jazz Festival

When: June/July

What: Not really a festival proper, the Jazz Fest is more like a whole bunch of concerts (held at various downtown venues) concentrated during ten days.

folk clubs

The Calgary and Canmore folk festivals are summer institutions, but what to do during the winter months? Thank your lucky stars for Calgary's longstanding folk clubs, that's what. (Okay, some of 'em prefer to be called "music clubs" now so as to properly reflect contemporary "folk" music's more-than-Bob-Dylan scope, but you know what I mean.)

Bow Valley Music Club

Established: 1992
Where: Strathcona Park Community Centre, 277 Strathcona Drive SW, 287-2299
House band: Coyote Moon
Recent acts: The Wyrd Sisters, Blackie and The Rodeo Kings

Calgary Folk Club

Established: 1971
Where: Dalhousie Community Centre, 5432 Dalhart Road NW, 286-5651
House band: Wild Colonial Boys
Recent acts: Austin Lounge Lizards, Barra MacNeils

Nickelodeon Music Club

Established: 1980
Where: Crescent Heights Community Hall, 1101-2nd St. NW, *284-5440*
Recent acts: Bill Bourne, Shari Ulrich

Rocky Mountain Folk Club

Established: 1975
Where: Hillhurst-Sunnyside Community Hall, 1320-5th Ave. NW, *244-2912*
House band: Ceard
Special event: In addition to the concert season, the RMFC holds an annual Robbie Burns Day blow-out that's almost as legendary as the man himself.

Carifest
When: June
What: Annual 10-day festival of all things Caribbean: dancing, food, arts, and a parade. More calypso/Soca/reggae than you can shake a stick at. Or your "booty," for that matter.

Shakespeare in the Park
When: July to August
What: A longtime summer tradition in which a Mount Royal College troupe stages free Willy plays on Prince's Island. Performances usually run for six nights of the week.

Word on the Street
When: last Sunday in September
What: Part of a nationwide up-with-literacy initiative, Word on the Street is a one-day book/magazine fair held at Eau Claire Market. Big names read from the mainstage, while other authors chat it up at smaller tents.

Cool shoes and fresh fish. Late-night television wonder products and steak from the back of a van. Psychic advice and slave labour. Customized wrestling masks and, uhmm, *more* customized wrestling masks. The following chapter will help that paycheque evaporate faster than usual.

Secret Service

Unlisted phone numbers are a dime a dozen. Nemesis International is so secret that even if you manage to locate their number, the receptionist answers the phone using a fake name. With so much anti-advertising in place, it's a miracle anyone can get close enough to hire their services (let alone squeeze off a prank phone-call). Business, however, is very good: Nemesis International deals in corporate counter-espionage. Is someone eavesdropping on your crucial oilpatch merger? Hacking into your mainframe? Nemesis will set things straight. (Don't call them, they'll find you.) The team of six investigators, all with private investigation and/or law enforcement backgrounds, operate out of an unmarked (what did you expect?) southeast Calgary office building. Nemesis has debugged over a million square feet of downtown office space, sweeping buildings with radio-frequency detectors and x-raying walls for concealed recording devices. They've uncovered everything from hi-tech laser microphones to – would you believe? – jerryrigged baby monitors.

Leather Report

The annual "Secret Santa" gift exchange at your office need no longer be a source of "What to buy?" anxiety. B&B Emporium (426-8th Ave. SE, 265-7789) offers a wide variety of gift-giving ideas: nipple clamps, benwa balls, riding crops, dildos, maid uniforms, thigh-high boots, etc. They also stock vintage "violet wands," an arcane early-electrical device designed to (cough) cure what ails ya. (Even kinkier: Teletubbies head gear.) The store carries a wide selection of rubber garments and adult-sized infant wear (don't ask), and crafts customized leather fetish gear. They'll even do up wrestling masks in the fabric of your choice. B&B's close proximity to City Hall may seem weird, but without naming names let's just say certain lunch-hour shoppers find the location rather . . . *convenient.* Shocking Fact: the wedding dress in the front window took home a ribbon at the Stampede craft show.

Give Daddy His Arm Back, Little Fishy

Like it or not, the "value-added experience" is here to stay. Whether it's book superstores with in-house cafés or VIP rooms at movie theatres, it's not enough to simply sell a product anymore – you gotta offer that extra oomph. At Big Al's Aquarium Services (*8228 Macleod Tr. S, 640-0635*), you can witness a bloody feeding frenzy while shopping for a new guppy net. (No, I'm not talking about a "half-off" sale.) Every Tuesday at 7 p.m. the public is invited to watch Big Al's sharks (one "lemon" and two "nurses," each about three feet long) chow down on mackerel and squid. Keep your fingers away from the tank and repeat after me: "This was no boating accident!"

Secret Sale

Twice a year (October and April), the University of Calgary sells off used sporting equipment. Items include bikes, boats, and tents – all of which is former rental equipment, so prices vary according to wear 'n' tear. Worth checking out, but take a pass on the jockstraps.

cyber cafés

Thanks to the wonders of technology, you can now check e-mail while drinking coffee.

Cyber Club Café
1910A-37th St. SW, 242-3965
$3 for 30 min., $5 for 60 min.

Screenplay Café
37th St. and Richmond Rd. SW, 246-8750
$5 for 30 min., $7.50 for 60 min.

Virtual Reality Café
26 Crowfoot Terrace NW, 208-8787
$12 for 60 min., 10% discount with $5 lifetime membership

Wired - The Cyber Café
1032-17th Ave. SW, 244-7070
$2.50 for 15 min.

specialty video

When the local Blockbuster just won't cut it.

Little Saigon Video
2G, 4710-17th Ave. SE, 248-2022

Richard's Video Latino
1177-11th Ave. SW, 245-8367

Thuy Vietnamese Video Rentals
21, 2936 Radcliffe Rd. SE, 273-8255

Video & Sound (Chinese)
116-16th Ave. NW, 266-0217

high fashion

Some sartorial experts believe that clothing made from hemp will lead the wearer down a slippery slope, culminating in garments made from cocaine and heroin. Consider yourself warned.

Grass Roots
112-10th St. NW, 270-2193

The Hemporium
926A-17th Ave. SW, 245-3155

Secret Economy

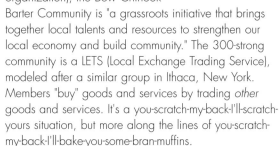

Call it anti-shopping. A project of the Arusha Centre (a non-profit development education organization), the Bow Chinook Barter Community is "a grassroots initiative that brings together local talents and resources to strengthen our local economy and build community." The 300-strong community is a LETS (Local Exchange Trading Service), modeled after a similar group in Ithaca, New York. Members "buy" goods and services by trading *other* goods and services. It's a you-scratch-my-back-I'll-scratch-yours situation, but more along the lines of you-scratch-my-back-I'll-bake-you-some-bran-muffins.

The *Bow Chinook Barter Bulletin* runs ads for available goods and services: babysitting, herbal therapeutic packs, speech pathology, friendship (honest!), CD burning, cooking, cleaning, data entry, skating lessons, web-page design, dry bean soups, farm-fresh beef, jewelry, hedge trimming, and beyond. Several local businesses (including Self-Connection Books, Trend Clothing, and Dragon's Den Martial Arts Supplies) are also in on the action.

The Bow Chinook Barter Community (*233-10th St. NW, 270-8002*) is currently negotiating a deal with Calgary Transit involving non-peak service. At press time, it was not known whether the plan involved pushing buses up hills.

retail playground of the stars

A celebrity and her/his money are soon parted. Here's the skinny on recent brushes with fame.

Crown Surplus

1005-11th St. SE, 265-1754
What: Specialists in all things military, Crown Surplus was selling cargo pants before they were cool. (Note: aforementioned pants may very well be "uncool" by the time you read this.)
Celebrity client: Cher
Purchase: sleeveless German Army underwear tops ("singlets") for herself, jackets and shirts for son Elijiah Blue.
Trivia: Cher shopped for a hour, spent a couple hundred bucks.

Yogya

2525-16th St. SE, 264-4966
What: Yogya imports fine furniture, etc. from the Jakarta area.
Celebrity clients: David Bowie and Iman
Purchase: "a couple of small things"
Trivia: The jetsetting couple live in Indonesia part-time, so rest assured they know their Indo-stuff.

Starbucks

723-17th Ave. SW, 209-2888
What: duh
Celebrity client: Neve Campbell
Purchase: black coffee, but she brought her own smokes
Trivia: Other 17th Ave. Starbucks celeb sightings (unconfirmed) include Ice-T, John Goodman, and Bill Pullman. But not all at the same time.

newsstands

More than just the usual 7-Eleven fare, newsstands offer a wealth of out-of-town newspapers, foreign and specialty mags, and general weird stuff. (Who knew there were so many biker magazines?) Warning: these are not libraries.

Billy's News & Smoke Shop
206-7th Ave. SW, 262-2894

Daily Globe News
1004-17th Ave. SW, 244-2060

Harry's News & Tobacco Shop
111-8th Ave. SW, 262-7938

With The Times
2212-4th St. SW, 244-8020
118-10th St. SW, 283-9257

**World News &
Dollar Plus Store**
220B-7th Ave. SW, 294-9441

recorded music

The legendary Record Store (that was the name, honest) may be dead and buried, but Calgary is still blessed with a handful of swell independent record stores:

Fidelio Records
Mount Royal Village, 229-9209
Classical (including 20th century work) and some jazz.

Feroshus
11, 718-17th Ave. SW
CDs/singles/albums in the house/techno/progressive vein. Plus: mix-tapes, club gear, and DJ equipment

Megatunes
#101, 932-17th Ave. SW, 229-3022
Jazz, "alternative," and especially good for blues & roots.

Melodiya
252A-17th Ave. SW, 246-8916
Melodiya is a skinny room packed with CDs and vinyl. Think indie, think midday CJSW. Videos and zines, too.

Sloth
1304-4th St. SW (basement), 265-6585
Similar deal to Melodiya, but bigger and with more used stuff. Tonnes of seven-inch singles.

psychics galore

Plagued with bad vibes, but don't like the idea of psychic counseling over a long-distance phone connection? There's plenty of cosmic help to be had in town. A sampling:

Destiny
281-9008
It seems a bit weird that someone called "Destiny" would use your *legal* name to whip up a psychic analysis, but the world's a mysterious place. $50/hour will get you a 9-year cycle reading, and perhaps some palmistry to boot.

Kindred Spirits
2002-33rd Ave. SW, 686-9449
Pat Owens and Paula Moore run this gift shoppe/psychic parlour. Come for the tea cup readings, stay for the angel paraphernalia.

Lawrence Grodsky
229-3700
He's billed as the "Master Psychic With Love," so you know you're in good hands. (Perhaps it's irresponsible of me to use "love" and "hands" in the same sentence. Larry's not that kind of psychic.)

Moneca Tremblay
228-6499 or 253-9328
A French-Canadian ESP consultant, Moneca uses her powers (and your birthday) to craft a "life cycle" reading. Also does ear candling.

Nora Osborne
Get the cosmic skinny from a professional psychic who started out reading beer foam (*à la* tea leaves). Nora used to holds courts on Wednesday nights at Victoria's Restaurant, but only the planets know whether she'll return.

Run by a transplanted Israeli DJ named Armand, Recordland (*1208-9th Ave. SE, 262-3839*) attracts local yokels and visiting superstars alike with its thousands-strong collection of used LPs. While the ever-present Led Zeppelin/reggae tunes blast from the cashier stereo, musicheads teeter on upturned milk crates, straining to reach tightly-packed top shelves. Local DJs root through the funk, soul, and sound effects sections, always on the prowl for a fresh sample. Obsessive music maniacs like Radiohead and Pavement flip out when they find long-sought-after rare gems – and these are guys who record-hunt all over the world.

The Inglewood store does a tidy used CD business and has started to stock a small supply of new vinyl, but it remains *the* place to nab obscure jazz sides or a copy of The Stones' *Their Satanic Majesties Request* with original 3D cover. (It's cheap, too, with most discs selling in the $5-$10 range.) The store's semi-wonky classifications range from hypnotism and warbling movie stars to Winston Churchill speeches and "nude covers" (the last two are separate categories, thank goodness). A successful trip requires diligence, but there's no telling what you can dig up over the course of an hour or five. Diehard Recordlanders sift through the "new" piles on an almost daily basis, and with good reason: Armand is constantly sitting at his desk, cleaning a newly acquired stack o' wax. He says he's got a million records in storage, and judging by the store's speedy turnover, the man speaketh the truth.

for sale: unusual musical instruments

Domba – All Things African
270-7871

One World African & Latin Drum Company
217-6790

Macen Accordion Studio
2614 Centre St. N, 277-7050

cooking supplies

Still eating baked beans out of the can? With a old McDonald's coffee stir-stick? Good grief.

B J Restaurant Equipment Supplies
1101 Centre St. NW, 230-0039
From woks to stock-pots, with ladles for good measure.

The Compleat Cook
Bankers Hall, 264-0449
Dalhousie Station, 286-5220
Willowpark Village, 278-1220
Cookware! Dinnerware! Bakeware! Pretty much any "ware" you could possibly think of.

Hing Wah Imports
312 Centre St. S, 264-1542
Rice cookers and steamer baskets at must-sell prices.

Russell Food Equipment Ltd.
5707-4th St. SE, 253-1383
Super-pro cooking equipment (knives, spoons, ranges) served up in a bare-bones environment.

farmers markets

Alberta law dictates that 80 percent of vendors must "make, bake, or grow" their products to constitute a bona fide Farmers Market. (Even so, less honourable fiends will still try to slip commercial produce into the mix. *Caveat eator.*) From traditional beets-beans-broccoli fare to farm-raised trout (not to mention the circus-like atmosphere), FMs are always worth a gander:

Bearspaw Lions Farmers Market

One kilometre west of city limits on Highway 1A
Sundays, noon to 4 p.m.

Blackfoot Market

5600-11th St. SE
Fridays & Saturdays, 8 a.m. to 5 p.m.
Sundays, 10 a.m. to 4 p.m.

Crossroads Market

16th Ave & Barlow Tr. NE
Fridays to Sundays, 8 a.m. to 6 p.m.

Calgary Grassroots Northland Market

Northland Village Mall parking lot (NW)
Tuesdays, 4 to 8 p.m.

Calgary Hillhurst Sunnyside Market

12250-5th Ave. NW
Wednesdays, 4 to 8 p.m.

Millarville Farmers Market

Millarville Racetrack, south of city limits on Highway 22
Saturdays, 8:30 a.m. to noon

pole to pole

Mondo Canuck called Gary Burns' *The Suburbanators* "the most promising first feature by a Canadian director to come along in years." What's more, the flick is a time-capsule tour of some dearly-departed Calgary barbershops. (A moment of silence for Jim's on 17th Ave.) They're going fast, but there's still a handful of classic striped-pole chopshops left in town. A sampling of the best follows, including two establishments still offering the straight-razor shave (an HIV-queasy no-no at most places these days).

Wally's Barber Shop

1603-9th St. SW, 228-5662
Wally sold the joint a few months back so I can't vouch for its current condition, but in its heyday this two-seater was a classic. Wally and his sideman-of-the-moment would B.S. themselves into a frenzy, arguing about important things like who's spent the most time in Hawaii.
Haircut: $15
Shave: not on your life

Chinook Barber & Styling

Chinook Centre
Tucked in the basement, across the hall from the bowling alley, this is a little slice of '60s mall heaven. (The old-school effect was stronger before the public library became a police station, but them's the breaks.) The place doesn't look like its changed much over the years, save the early-'80s "style suggestions" above the mirrors.
Haircut: $12
Shave: yeah right

European Barber Shop

next door to the St. Louis Hotel
The European is a no-frills, one-chair room run by super-friendly Samuel. Decor highlights include the autograph-ed 8x10 glossies of strippers and a large sign adver-tising legal aid.
Haircuts: $10
Shave: $8

meat markets

A great place for lonely people to make new — whoops, wrong "meat market." Anyway, it's no surprise that the heart of Cattle Country boasts a multitude of butcher shops. Below are a few establishments offering a little more than steaks as thick as your arm. But they have that, too.

Bon Ton Meat Market
10, 1941 Uxbridge Dr. NW, 282-3132
140, 10233 Elbow Dr. SW, 640-4184
The best in Alberta beef/lamb/pork since 1921. (Free-range poultry, too.) Bon Ton is famous for their meat pies: steak and kidney, chicken, pork, beef, Tortiere, steak and mushroom, Scotch pie, and turkey.

Calgary Meats and Deli
1204 Edmonton Tr. NE, 276-1423
Traditional German and Swiss sausages and cold-cuts.

European Delicatessen and Imports
2717-14th St. SW, 244-0570
Imported deli-fare (German, Swiss, Austrian) and in-house sausages.

Fourth St. Meats

2100-4th St. SW, 229-3661
Formerly Red Deer Lake Meats and Deli, but not associated with the *other* Red Deer Lake Meats on 26th Ave. SE. (It's confusing, I know.) In addition to their fresh meat counter, Fourth St. Meats specializes in beef jerky and chicken wings. Catering available. The store's deli boasts the best ham'n'cheese buns in the city.

Gordon's Fine Meats

Eau Claire Market, 234-7060
Specializing in over 200 variety of sausage (Katmandu Turkey, Ginger Chicken, and more). Plus: jerkies, pepperoni, and haggis.

MacEwans Meats

1137B-17th Ave. SW, 228-9999
Your British/Scottish connection: Haggis, Ayrshire bacon, white pudding, blood pudding, Scotch pies, etc.

Mad Russian Smoke House

515G-36th Ave. NE, 277-7847
Can a place called "Mad Russian Smoke House" possibly disappoint? Nyet.

Val Co Foods

3434-34th Ave. NE, 250-2999
Formerly "Meat Liquidators Ltd." (liquid meat?! — good call on the name-change, guys), Val Co sells discounted fresh meat. They also feature over 200 feet of frozen bargains. Their stock varies according to what they can get, mostly drawn from over-productions and other "opportunity buys."

Artistic Barber Shop

219-6th Ave. SE, 263-8626
A true old-timer, the Artistic was forced to relocate from the doomed Crown Building into the mainfloor of the traffic court plaza, and it shows: gorgeous vintage sinks, chairs, etc. unceremoniously bolted into a bare bones retail nook. Safety note: chatterbox Doug cuts a mean lid, but his constant craning to eyeball passing skirt can get freaky when he's waving the blade.
Haircut: $12
Shave: $10

pet services

Healthy

Animals have it good: we feed them, play with them, and then pick up their crap. What the world needs now more than ever is A1 Pooper Scoopin' (*277-POOP*). Claiming to be "#1 in the #2 business," A1 Pooper Scoopin' (that number again: *277-POOP*) charges according to the number of pets and the size of the area to be scooped. They don't do llamas.

Ailing

Is your crane down-for-the-count with an impacted gizzard? Get thee to the Calgary Caged & Exotic Pet Clinic (*3118-17th Ave. SW, 240-3577*), *the* place to take ailing reptiles, ferrets, rabbits, birds, and wildlife. In 13 years of business, they've handled everything from a 12-foot Burmese python to one-inch caterpillars. By appointment only.

Dead

Roy Rogers didn't have to part with his beloved Trigger, so why should you say goodbye to your faithful companion? There's a bunch of taxidermists in the naked city, but only one using freeze-drying technology: Angler's Taxidermy Ltd. (*295-7534*). Much in the way you or I would make fruit leather, Angler's uses a giant compressor to suck all the moisture from your dearly departed. Depending on corpse size and grease content (bears don't work so well), the process can take up to six months.

If freeze-drying's not the thing, consider the Country Club Pet Resort & Pet Memorial Park (936-5685), "the most dignified pet disposition available." Personally speaking, nothing spells "dignity" like a combination resort-slash-cemetery. (Say, that gives me an idea . . . get me Club Med on the blower, pronto!)

Mystery Meat

This one stays between you and me: let's say there's this hypothetical guy who drives around the city in a hypothetical van filled with hypothetical meat (sausages, roasts, chops – hypothetically speaking). And let's say if you're in the right place at the right time (you can set your clock by this character), he'll sell ya some prime cuts for a song. A sweet deal to be sure, if you don't have any qualms about buying perishables from some dude in a hotel bar. Whoops, did I just say "hotel bar"? I meant to say "somewhere." Keep it on the QT and not word one to Mr. Taxman.

UNG Crazy

When the gun shop at 1315 Edmonton Tr. NE transmogrified into a video store, the new owner was left to deal with the towering roadside G-U-N sign. A little elbow grease and some Scrabble-like brainwork later, and UNG Video was born. (Granted, you won't find "ung" in your Funk & Wagnall's, but. . . .) Not everyone is impressed with this feat of ingenuity; asked about the store's weird name, an UNG clerk simply shrugged.

Portugal's Finest Bakery Ltd.

2741-17th Ave. SW, 240-1962

Specializing in corn bread. Plus: cakes, pastries, deli meats, and other Portuguese products.

fishmongers

Living a million miles inland shouldn't prevent you from enjoying seafood without resorting to a can-opener. In addition to the following markets, don't forget about the refrigerated trucks occasionally parked along Crowchild and Macleod Trails. Curbside seafood — now *that's* good eatin'!

Atlantic Pacific Fish Market

201, 4909-17th Ave. SE, 235-5313

Billingsgate Fish Co.

630-7th Ave. SE, 571-7700

Bluenose Fish Co.

Eau Claire Market, 263-3474

Boyd's Lobster Shop

1515-14th St. SW, 245-6300

Portage Seafoods

8409 Elbow Dr. SW, 252-3930

Sakana Village

2, 1725 Centre St. N, 277-5533

Seafood Centre

183A, 1623 Centre St. N, 277-9417

Movie Mecca

By the time you read this, Video & Sound will have moved from its longtime Chinatown location to 1715 Centre St. NW. (Something about their building being leveled for a parking lot.) Regardless, Video & Sound is still the best video store in town. (They're big into DVD and laser-disc, too.) The store's jam-packed shelves hold pretty much any movie you could want (and a lot you most certainly *don't* want), including straight-to-video and made-for-cable titles. You want more? How about: tonnes of animé and martial arts action, Chinese videos/DVDs, a wide selection of videos featuring real people getting really hurt (*Best of Extreme Catfighting*, *Faces of Death*, *Banned from TV*), and the borderline illegal (*Vancouver Voyeur* is a collection of change-room video cam footage). Video & Sound even sells the Pamela Anderson & Tommy Lee workout tape ($34.95). All that, plus it's open 'til 1 a.m. every night.

Book 'Em Benny

The Calgary Philharmonic Orchestra's annual used-book fundraiser (a.k.a. "Benny the Bookworm") is a reader's delight. The books are in great shape and sell for peanuts (50¢ paperbacks, and the like), so it's advisable to get there earlier than later. The 'worm usually runs for a Fri-Sat-Sun weekend in May. Locations vary, but it's pretty much always at a mall. Students of the English Lit variety are advised to take note: the books are all donated to the CPO, so you never know exactly what's in store, but there's always a load of literature (and not just the classics). If you know your Fall/Winter semester in advance, it's possible to score a year's worth of texts for the cost of a cheap lunch.

Secret Labour

Rain gutters to clean? Heavy stuff to lift? Whether you're overworked or simply feeble, head on down to Centre St. S (*between 12th and 13th Aves.*) and snag your own personal Spartacus. With bagged lunches in one hand and cups of A&W coffee in the other, strong-backed gents start gathering on the street before the cock crows, eager to hop in the box of a passing pick-up and earn some under-the-table coin.

(Note: the ladies who mill around the opposite side of the street will do many interesting things for money, but hanging drywall ain't one of 'em.)

Happiness is a Used Sink

Preferring the term "recycler" to "scavenger," Harry Bona roots through soon-to-be-demolished buildings, buying up anything he thinks he can sell: hardwood flooring, tin roofs (perfect for sundaes), beams, entire garages, lighting fixtures, etc. Harry's empire started in Winnipeg, followed by a Calgary location (*125-61st Ave. SE, 255-9505*). The Happy One now has salvage yards across the country; he trucks his treasures from one city to another, so it's a real crapshoot as to what you'll find on any given day. Happy Harry's — when you care enough to renovate your basement with a pink toilet salvaged from a Winnipeg bingo parlour.

healthy foodstuffs

Vitamins, free-range critters, organic greens, etc. Today is the first day of the rest of your life, so wipe that bacon grease off your chin and step to it.

Amaranth Whole Foods
730, 20 Crowfoot Cr. NW, 547-6333

Blueberry Creek Natural Food
330-10th St. NW, 283-8970

Bowness Health Food
6435 Bowness Rd. NW, 286-2224

Community Natural Foods
1304-10th Ave. SW, 229-2383

Nature's Fresh Market
14, 11625 Elbow Dr. SW, 281-8957

Rainbow Vitamins
4, 2015 - 4th St. SW, 245-3944

Sunnyside Market
10, 338-10th St. NW, 270-7477

Sunrise Natural Foods & Spices
107, 920-36th St. NE

Vitamins First
2136-33rd Ave. SW, 242-1777

The '90s were cruel to a lot of city shopping malls, transforming them into gloomy Loonie Store wastelands. Overrun by empty storefronts and marauding packs of seniors, certain once-flashy complexes now feel like an outtake from *Mad Max Goes Suburban*. The only upside to the gloom is TV Showcase, a chain of shops devoted to selling only "as seen on television" products. (Hey, as long as they pay the rent. . . .) Located in the Marlborough, Sunridge, North Hill and Northland Village malls, TV Showcase is like a really good *SCTV* sketch: food dehydrators, the "massage" steering-wheel cover, a rainbow of miracle mops, etc. Heck, there's so many "miracle" products that one wonders whether The Pope is called in to do inventory. All the big names are here, including The Juiceman II, The Amazing New Heat Magic Microwavable Hot Plate, and "Banjo: The World's First Genetic Response Fishing Lure." (I have no idea what "genetic response" refers to, but it's been marked down to $39.99 so shake a leg.) Inside the store, dueling VCRs blast *The Best of Just Kidding Volumes 1 & 2* ("the most hysterical gags and practical jokes ever caught on video," $34.99) and Suzanne Somers' bubbly ThighMaster testimony ("I love the burn you get when you're squeezing" – hmmm, maybe she's misusing The Juiceman II), making for a late-night sensory overload in broad daylight. But wait, there's more! Act now and you'll receive: a touch-activated Shark Snack Bowl (it plays the *Jaws* theme while you fish around for that last Cheezie, $29.99), the "new" Perm For-A-Day (totally kicks on the "old" Perm-For-A-Day, $14.99), and Blue Shield Total Protection Fashion Eyewear ($4.99) for the entire family. As an added bonus, TV Showcase also stocks a swelegant selection of videos, including Jerry Springer highlights, hilarious mid-air collisions, and cute baby animals tumbling down grassy slopes. In a word, wow.

SLEEPLESS IN DRAGON CITY

Chinatown seems all formal and proper on the surface, but a little digging yields smutty delights. Lee's Oriental Arts is a good example. The tiny shop, found on the main floor of Dragon City *(328 Centre St. S)*, gives off a wholesome *feng shui* vibe — until you look carefully inside the glass display cases. Mixed in amongst the G-rated artwork are statuettes of amourous couples engaged in, er, compromising positions. We all know that size doesn't matter in such situations, except when it comes to money: small statues are $28, large are an extra 30 bucks.

Oooh, Ahhh ... Fashion

Aluminum Planet

Eaton's Centre, 262-0048
"Fashion-forward street wear" for trendy boys and girls: Storm, Fresh Jive, Luscious, Lithium, Travel Gear, Label Whore, Puma.

Blue Light Special

926-17th Ave. SW, 245-5338
Street wear, accessories, jewelry, and watches for the "thirteen to thirty" set. Not your usual mall fare, Blue Light carries a lot of stuff by local designers. As far as name-brands go: Flo, 3 Stones, Sugar. For men and women.

Brooklyn Clothing Company

201, 1211 Kensington Rd. NW, 283-4006
Specializing in European denim and California shirt-wear for the discerning gentleman: Diesel, Big Star, Replay, St,ssy. And Fluevogs to boot.

Divine

720-17th Ave. SW, 228-2540
"Club wear" for the body, and Chuck Taylors/Doc Martens/Swear for the feet.

Focus Clothing

800-16th Ave. SW, 244-4426
Women's fashions: Betsey Johnson, Misura, Teenflo, In Wear, Virani, Francomirabelli, Laundry by Shelli Segal.

Fritz Lang

722-11th Ave. SW, 234-8607
Dolce & Gabbana, Comme des Garçons, Stone Island, Paul Smith, John Rocha, and Hugo – for gents and ladies both.

thrift stores

Some dedicated thrifters swear by the north Value Village (less picked-over than the south store), others settle for nothing less than the Red Deer VV. That may sound a touch fanatical, but ya burns the gas and ya takes your chances. Everyone's got their own standards and superstitions, but there's only one tried 'n' true thrift store rule: it's always hit and miss.

Interfaith Thrift Stores
8607-48th Ave. NW, 247-1146
1302-4th St. SW, 264-6372
4803-17th Ave. SE, 273-7848
130, 1935-37th St. SW, 242-1794
18, 6624 Centre St. S, 640-4996
8419 Elbow Dr. SW, 259-5925
6672-4th St. NE, 295-1201
1027, 3709-26th Ave. NE, 280-1188

IODE Bargain Shop
1318-1st St. SW, 266-6855

**Next To New
(Junior League of Calgary)**
511-22nd Ave. SW, 244-5355

Salvation Army Thrift Stores

133-5th Ave. SE, 262-2759

3012-17th Ave. SE, 235-3976

9919 Fairmount Dr. SE, 225-0087

3508-32nd Ave. NE, 735-3200

2880 Glenmore Tr. SE, 279-9035

Women In Need Thrift Stores

1403-14th St. SW, 245-1556

6432 Bowness Rd. NW, 288-4825

1919-32st St. SW, 569-7755

541, 3516-8th Ave. NE, 248-9696

2909 Richmond Rd. SW, 242-4969

Holt Renfrew

Eaton's Centre, 269-7341
New York's 5th Ave. meets Calgary's 8th Ave.: Prada, Chanel, Tiffany's, Gucci, Dolce & Gabbana, Max Mara, St. John, Louis Seraud, Donna Karan. . . . Cosmetics, too: Kiehl's, Smashbox, Prescriptives, Bobbi Brown, Sisley, La Prairie.

Oxygen

312 Bankers Hall, 264-5281
Men/Women
High-end his 'n' her urban sportswear: Versace Jeans Couture, Dolce & Gabbana Jeans, Kenneth Cole (the clothing, not the shoes). Some footwear (Fluevog, Campers).

Primitive

The Kensington location *(332-1̃0th St. NW, 270-8490)* sells Canadian designs by David Bitton and Lino Catalano. Plus: Free People, Bulldog, Rugby, Rudsack, Sinequanoné (Paris) and Custo (Barcelona). Ditto for the Mt. Royal store *(814-16th Ave. SW, 244-4404)*, but more evening and professional wear.

Purr

919-17th Ave. SW, 244-7877
Specializing in men's and ladies' shoes: Rocket Dog, Puma, Diesel, Swear. The sister store to Blue Light Special, Purr offers exclusive fashion from Smoking Lily (silk skirts, bags, and T-shirts from Victoria) and Custo (hand-painted shirts from Barcelona). Plus: home accessories, designer pillows, etc.

Sagesse Clothing Co.

801-17th Ave. SW, 229-0200
Men's and women's consignment fashions upstairs, new fem-stuff downstairs: Dex Bros, Itsus, Atricot, Powerline.

The Source

930-17th Ave. SW, 228-9112
124-10th St. NW, 270-3719
You've seen those damn Source stickers plastered all

over town, so you might as well own the T-shirt ($24). In addition to all the top-name skate/snowboards, The Source sells clothing (Fresh Jive, Drawers), shoes (DC, Etnie), and sunglasses (Arnette, Spy, Dragon).

Splash of Fashion

200, 1211 Kensington Rd. NW, 283-3353
Extensive jeanswear for the ladies (Big Star, Replay, Diesel, Miss Sixty). Plus: BCBG, Betsey Johnson, Camici, Poleci, Fluevog, etc.

Absolutely Diapers

634A-17th Ave. SW, 244-4449
Say what you will, but it's a look.

vintage clothing

Blue Light Special

926-17th Ave. SW, 245-5454
The main floor is new stuff, but there's vintage clothing (mostly '60s and '70s) and secondhand street-wear in the basement.

Deja-Vu Clothing

340-21st Ave. SW, 229-0100
Located in a heritage duplex boarding-house, Deja-Vu is the complete retro package. The store defines "vintage" as anything 25 years and older, and also sells shoes, purses, hats, collectibles, and antiques.

Divine

720-17th Ave. SW, 228-2540
Jeans, track suits, lime-green pantsuits, those sweaters with the little alligators on 'em, etc.

Polka Dots and Moonbeams

1227-9th Ave. SE, 262-0041
Large, rambling Inglewood shop jammed with men's and women's clothing, but specializing in dresses. Some Victorian and 1920s fashions, but mostly '40s to contemporary. Lots of accessories and jewelry, both new and vintage.

bookstores

The mega-bookstores have hit Calgary like a mid-July snowstorm. (Note to out-of-towners: that means they're all over the place.) And yeah, I'll admit there's something appealing about a giant store full of thousands of books (and the freedom to spill coffee on all of 'em), but the city's indie booksellers have got a good thing going, both new and used:

Another Dimension
This Kensington mainstay has been peddling "funny books" for years. Remember: comics aren't for kids anymore - they're too damn expensive. *324-10th St. NW, 283-7078*

Author Author
Used books in good shape, always worth a gander. *223-10th St. NW, 283-9521*

Best Little Wordhouse In The West
Same deal as above. Makes sense, since they used to share an owner. *911-17th Ave. SW, 245-6407*

Books & Books
This is one time when a small selection is a huge asset. Books & Books has the shelf space to showcase its off-the-beaten-path inventory, highlighting gems that would get lost in a mega-super-duper environment. *738A-17th Ave. SW, 228-3337.*

Cookbook Co. Cooks

No offense intended, but if you can't figure out what's going on here you probably can't even make toast. Lots of fancy hot sauces and other grocery delicacies for sale, too. And did I mention the winetasting and cooking classes? *722-11th Ave. SW, 265-6066.*

De Mille Technical Books

Evelyn De Mille opened this institution in 1956, the city's first store devoted solely to books. (As opposed to a book section in, say, a stationery shop.) Originally devoted to oilpatch-related reading, the store now handles tomes on everything from architecture to risk-management. *815-8th Ave. SW, 264-7411.*

Fair's Fair

Fair's Fair plows through boxloads of used books in any given day, and is a great place to snag discarded review copies of just-released — or even soon-to-be-released — books. (Hope this doesn't get anyone in trouble.) Two locations: *1430, 1609-14th St. SW, 245-2778 and 907-9th Ave. SE, 237-8156.*

Maptown

From travel guides to travel pillows. And, yes, maps. *100, 400-5th Ave. SW, 266-2241.*

consignment and second-hand

The following shops accept only the best in "previously -enjoyed" fashion. Sweat stains need not apply.

Changes
202, 2136-33rd Ave. SW, 240-3392

Changes Too
206, 4625 Varsity Dr. NW, 247-9434

Changes III
(are you seeing a pattern here?) *WillowPark Village, 225-2445* All three Changes have very particular criteria for accepting woman's clothing and accessories: high-end labels only, and nothing more than three years old.

The Pendulum
The north store (1802-1st St. NW, 276-6886) is all women's consignment fashion: Gap, InWear, Focus, Jacob. The Inglewood location *(1222-9th Ave. SE, 266-6369)* has both men's and women's clothing, as well as furniture from Indonesia and India.

Sagesse
801-17th Ave. SW, 229-0200
Consignment clothes and shoes for men and women. If it's still "in" and not threadbare, chances are Sagesse will want it.

Second Time Around Clothing
1804-1st NW, 276-6970
Children's clothes (including shoes) and maternity wear. Plus: toys and baby equipment.

Vespucci
6511 Elbow Dr. SW, 252-9558
810B-16th Ave. SW, 228-5166
High-end women's consignment fashion, shoes, and accessories.

army surplus

If you're looking for something in green that's inexpensive and wears like iron, army surplus is the way to go. An Arctic-issue parka (complete with felt-lined hood) will keep you warm no matter what mid-February decides to throw at us – and where else can you find clothing with cargo pockets? (Er, scratch that last bit.)

Crown Surplus

1005-11th St. SE, 265-1754
All the big armies are represented at this Inglewood institution: American, Canadian, Sweden, Norway, Germany, France, Italian, et al.

Quinn The Eskimo

538-9th Ave. SE, 234-0466
Parkas, dud grenades, gas masks, and clothing from Armies the world over.

The Soldier Shop

129B-17th Ave. SE, 229-4270
Clothing, collectibles, firearms, ammunition, webbing, and the whole nine yards. Lots of Canadian and British items.

Off The Wall
There's no telling what used treasures you can find here, as long as you're willing to: (a) excavate, and (b) move aside the occasional sleeping cat. *2042-4th Ave. SW, 229-3066.*

Pages On Kensington
Two floors of book action (both fiction and non) located next to the Plaza Theatre. *1135 Kensington Rd. SW, 283-6655.*

Phoenix Comics
Everything from standard men-in-tights fare to jaded indie hepcat faves. Lots of models and toys to boot, as one would expect from a building emblazoned with a giant Silver Surfer mural. *2523A-17th Ave. SW, 246-1706*

R.J. Sinden
Hardboiled paperbacks and fine art: two great tastes that taste great together. *1336-9th Ave. SE, 263-5885.*

Librairie Monette

Specializing in French books, music, and videos, Librairie Monette has a certain *je ne sais what* which I just can't put my finger on. *817-17th Ave. SW (upstairs), 244-6433.*

The Sentry Box

More sci-fi and fantasy books than William Shatner has tribbles, if that make any sense whatsoever. I don't think it does. *1835-10th Ave. SW, 245-2121.*

Self Connection Books

Billed as "Books For Conscious Living," Self Connection covers spirituality, alternative lifestyles, health, parenting, nutrition, and beyond. *4004-19th St. NW, 284-1486.*

Shakespeare's Shelf

Immaculate used books; especially good for literature. *201, 1019-17th Ave. SW, 245-2440*

A Woman's Place Bookstore

Health, self-development, addictions, women's and men's studies, and fiction. *Main Floor, 1412 Centre St. S, 263-5256.*

Grow Operation

Firmly established in Europe and Japan, the idea of "Community Supported Agriculture" is making headway in North America. CSAs basically cut out the middle man and help spread the burden of agricultural risk-taking, long the sole responsibility of the farmer: consumers buy shares in a farm, then pick up their cut of the harvest directly from the farmer. For the consumer, it's not as reliable as popping over to the mega-mart (no rain, after all, means no food), but there's a warm/fuzzy feeling that results from sticking it to The Man – and the produce generally kicks on any store-bought chemi-grow. There are now more than 30 CSAs in Canada, including Kris Vester's Blue Mountain Bio-Dynamic Farms *(Carstairs, 337-2496)*. Vester's mandate is to build a healthy relationship between producers and consumers, and if the corporate monopoly gets smashed in the process, that's a nice bonus. After buying into Blue Mountain – $175 for a half-share (which should feed two people), $350 for a full – the next step is to rendezvous with Farmer Kris at the Sunnyside Farmer's Market (Sunnyside Community Centre) every Wednesday between noon and 8 p.m. He'll load you up with a boxful of that week's particular haul (according to season), and then it's *bon appetit*. Note: Blue Mountain also offers a "work discount" if you're willing to lend some elbow grease.

Gathering Places

Pop quiz: What's weirder, witches on Nose Hill or Buddhists in Ogden?
Read the following chapter, then cast your ballot. And if you're stumped
for an answer (and the UFO people aren't being any help),
you can always play chess instead.

God Milk?

Ray Sharma's NW home became an overnight pilgrimage sensation when two brass Lord Ganesha statues began "drinking" milk from spoons. The milk would seemingly disappear into Ganesha's elephant-like trunk, then slowly pool around the statue's base. The occurrence was part of a larger statues-drinking-milk phenomena which swept the world in 1995, thought to signal Ganesha's earthly reincarnation. Pediatricians believe Ganesha has since progressed to solids.

UFO Research Association, Phone Home

St. Paul, Alberta may boast a 12-metre high UFO landing pad, but Calgary is home to the UFO Research Association. Or perhaps I should say "Calgary *was* home to the UFO Research Association." The researchers aren't returning phone messages and – at the risk of sounding like their mother(ship) – they never write and never call. Did they get too close to the truth? Or just too close to an alien probe? We may never know the awful facts, but at least we still have the St. Paul Chamber of Commerce and UFO Sightings Hotline: 1-888-733-8367.

Got No Time

Opened in September 1915, the Balmoral School has it all: Ionic pilasters, carved lion heads – and no clock in its clock tower. Nobody can nail down the reason, but some claim an elaborate clock was purchased from a British factory . . . and shipped on the *Titanic*.

There's no sexy folklore behind the old Utilities Building (the 100 block of 6th Ave. SW). Here's the scoop: no money, no clock, end of story. There is, however, a big circle where a clock would fit rather nicely.

Secret Park

What evil lurks beneath the waters of the Glenmore Reservoir? Probably none, but there *is* an old picnic area. The park was a popular destination for leisure-loving locals until it was submerged underneath 1.5 square miles of quality H_2O in 1933. Attendance really dropped off after that. Go figure.

high societies

As the following list proves, societies and clubs offer something for everyone. The saddest, most friendless wallflower should be able to find a kindred spirit, even if they have to lie about their personality to do so.

Alberta Horseshoe Pitchers Association
280-2379
Since the dissolution of the Alberta Handgrenade Pitchers Association, this is now the only place where "close" counts. Membership: $10/yr.

Alberta Skeptics
P.O. Box 5571, Station A, T2H 1X9
They claim to a society of open-minded people who are "cautious in drawing conclusions," but I doubt it.

Alexandra Writers' Centre Society
922-9th Ave. SE, 264-4730
A supportive environment for budding scribblers, like a writer's womb.

Bow Valley *Megaloponera Foetens* Appreciation Society
Box 1103, Station M, T2P 2K9, 229-9661
An organization dedicated to "totally grooving on the excellent vibes of the Cameroonian stink ant." Whatever.

Calgary Canary Club
7816 Hunterburn Hill NW, 274-1092
Mainly a canary show club, but they do take the occasional field-trip to local coalmines. (Joke!) Publishers of the "Chirps" newsletter.

Calgary Doll Club
P.O. Box 28, 4404-12th St. NE, T2E 6K9
Have you seen that movie *Child's Play?* 'Nuff said.

Calgary Numismatic Society
244-4047
Numismatics often experience difficulty breathing, and have to carry an inhaler at all times — whoops, that's *asthmatics*. Numismatics simply enjoy collecting money. Membership: $10/yr, preferably in small unmarked pre-Renaissance bills.

Canadian Association of Wooden Money Collectors
P.O. Box 2643, Station M, T2P 3C1
Nobody ever told these guys not to accept any wooden nickels. Membership: $10/yr, or a fistful of toothpicks.

Oooooh, Witchy Women

Haven't actually witnessed this firsthand, but . . . local Wiccan women (a.k.a. witches, but good witches) supposedly gather on Nose Hill every full moon, staking out special spots corresponding to the compass points. Hands are joined and everyone takes turns talking positively about negative things. (If I understand this correctly, a frustrated smoker would say something like "The thing I *love* most about myself is how I smoke like a godforsaken chimney. And my breath — whoa! Don't get me started about how much I *love* my nicotine breath.") The witches form two parallel lines, joining hands to form a tunnel. Everyone begins to make buzzing noises (this has something to with bees) and takes turns running thru the tunnel. Afterwards, they all go out for fries.

I may have some details confused. If so, I'm sorry and please don't turn me into a toad. Warning: I carry a bucketful of water with me at all times. (Ah, witch jokes never get tired, do they?)

Tower of Babble

A losing battle with Oakridge residents over an unsightly transmission spire has forced Cantel to get sneaky: the steeple atop the Bow Valley Christian Church (*5300-53rd Ave. NW*) is both a heavenly beacon and cleverly-disguised cell-phone communications tower. (The church cut a deal with Cantel to help foot their renovation bill.) From your salty sailor mouth to God's ear — something to keep in mind the next time you're considering a gridlocked phone-sex quickie.

Chess Mates

If you're searching for Bobby Fischer, keep searching. But if you're just looking for a game of chess, scoot over to Words Books & Cappuccino Bar *(1715-17th Ave. SW)*. For years, the bookstore has attracted strangers eager to square off on the 8x8, making it your best bet for finding a spur-of-the-moment opponent.

Other chess haunts include:

The Elephant & Castle Pub

8th Ave and 4th St. SW (Eaton Centre, downstairs)
The Calgary Chess Club meets for beer and battle every Tuesday at 7 p.m.

The Kerby Centre

113-7th Ave. SW
60+ players can drop-in on Wednesdays (9 a.m. 'til noon).

MacEwan Students Centre, University of Calgary

The U of C Chess Club meets Thursdays at 6 p.m. It's hit and miss, but you can always try the coffee shops for informal pick-up games: Terra Nova Café *(323A-17th Ave. SW)*, The Roasterie *(314-10th St. NW and 227-10th St. NW)*, and The Planet *(2212-4th St. SW)*.

Germans From Russia Heritage Society

Write to: *247 Huntridge Way NE, T2K 4C4*

Genealogy seminars, Oktoberfest, and sausage-making. Emigration has its privileges.

The Magic of Christmas

Box 48071, Midlake RPO, T2X 3C7, 243-0657

Since 1981, the club's mandate has been "to spread loving, caring, and sharing especially at Christmas." Jerks.

Singular Society of the Baker St. Dozen

Dedicated to the discussion and dissection of Sherlock Holmes mysteries. No contact info available at press-time, so you'll just have to put on your deerstalker and sniff 'em out.

Bottlescrew Bill's Old English Pub (140-10th Ave. SW, 263-7900) gives a whole new meaning to "armchair travel." For years, the pub has offered customers the taste sensation known as "Around The World In 80 Beers." Travellers are issued a passport (which records all the usual particulars, such as "Colour of Eyes: Red, Blotchy, or Dilated?"), and they're eligible to get busy drinking 80 different beers in 12 months. ("Around The World . . ." used to run the course of three months, but the pub found that things got a little, shall we say, *sloppy* – especially when the clock started running out and enthusiastic patrons had, like, 30 beers to down in a single evening.)

The 80 beers are selected from the pub's 200-plus menu, and come in cans, bottles, and on tap. (Some of 'em get pretty big, too: "Mississippi Mud" comes in a jug.) The globe is well-represented, with brews from Mexico, Australia, Trinidad, South Africa, England, Scotland, all over Europe and Asia, U.S., and Canada.

For the record, the travel itinerary is as follows: Bass, Boddingtons, Double Diamond, John Smiths, Newcastle Brown, Charles Wells IPA, Ruddles County, McEwen's Scotch Ale, McAndrew's Stock Ale, Tartan Bitter, Adventis Wheat Dopple Bock, Becks, Bitburger Pils, Erdinger Dunkel, Erdinger Weissbier, Holsten Festbock, Lowenbrau, Schneider Weisse, Warsteiner Pilsner, Chimary, Stella Artois, Tuborg, Faxe, Knonenbourg, "33" Export, Fischer Amber, Grolsch, Heineken, Moretti, Peroni, Ferdinand Premium, Pilsner Urquell, Okocim, Okocim Strong, Golden Pheasant, Caffrey's Irish Ale, Guinness Stout, Harp Lager, Kilkenny Cream Ale, Smithwicks Ale, Coopers Sparkling Ale, James Boag Lager, Steinlager, Tsingtao, Tiger, Asahi Super Dry, Kirin Ichiban, Kirin Lager, Sapporo Draft, Cass, Carib Lager, Castle Lager, Old Speckled Hen, Corona Extra, Dos Equis XX, Pacifico Clara, Sol, Mississippi Mud, Puerto Habana Lager, Stroh Bohemian, Alley Cat, Peak, Big Rock Grasshopper, Wild Horse, Brew Brothers, Shaftebury Brewing, Granville Island, Okanagan Spring, Tree Brewing, Tin Whistle, Creemore Springs Lager, Sleeman Honey Brown, Silver Creek Lager, Sleeman Dark, Seigneuriale, Seigneuriale Blonde, Unibroue Blanche de Chambly, Unibroue Eau Beuite, Unibroue la Fin du Monde, and Unibroue Maudite.

For the more laidback traveler, Bottlescrew Bill's also offers a leisurely Scotch tour: 32 malted delights, with no time limit.

Society of Kabalarians of Canada

2618 Richmond Rd. SW, 246-0926

Kabalarian philosophy espouses "constructive living based on principles of right thinking, right breathing, and right eating." Right on.

United Empire Loyalists' Association of Canada, Calgary Branch

830, 860 Midridge Dr. SE, 256-7458

The UELAC is dedicated to uniting "descendants of those families who, as a result of the American revolutionary war, sacrificed their homes in retaining their loyalty to the British Crown." Talk about holding a grudge.

Club Rendezvous bills itself as "a meeting place for open-minded couples," and that's all they're sayin' unless you buy a membership. The private, members-only club operates on Friday and Saturday nights; each night is, to use club lingo, a theme "party." Themes include: "Fleshdance," "Housecoat Party," "Sheer and See-Through," and "Lady in Red Night." Memberships cost $5/year for "associate" status (it'll cost you an additional $30 per "party") or $50/year for "full" membership. Full members only pay $20/party and also get to vote on club issues (use your imagination). Note: the club provides munchies and music, but it's a BYOB affair so as to circumvent those pesky liquor laws. Club Rendezvous doesn't give out its address to guys (I will tell you this: it's been at the same Ogden location for 12 years), but women can get the full scoop by calling 279-6830 between 8:30 and 9 p.m. on party nights.

Dog Parks

Officially known as "off-leash areas," dog parks are a great place to meet other pup-minded individuals. (It's a bit awkward to shake hands while wearing the ol' bread-bag oven-mitt, but. . . .) It's an ever-changing count (communities sometimes tire of the, shall we say, by-products), but Calgary has around 200 dog parks. Three of the biggest and most popular are:

Southland Natural Park

(where Anderson Rd. meets Deerfoot Tr., SE)

River Park

(Altadore, SW)

Nose Hill Park

(but only certain parts, NW)

Power to the People

Is the Amazing Presto's United Alternative not "alternative" enough for ya? Here are some revolutionary suggestions:

Food Not Bombs

Motto: "Hunger is an outrage." Food Not Bombs began in San Francisco, but chapters are sprouting up all over North America. ("Chapter" is really a misnomer since there's no governing body.) In Calgary, good-hearted punks collect food that would otherwise go to waste, cook up a big vegetarian spread, and then serve it to anyone who's hungry. The chow flows on Saturdays at 2 p.m. in Olympic Plaza. *266-8858.*

University of Calgary Revolutionary Anarchist Klub

A Students' Union-approved anarchy may sound like a contradiction, but these cats are serious about waving the black flag. (Well, as serious as anyone can be whose mission statement uses the word "funification.") The U of CRAK mandate is "to provide an outlet for creative Anarchism and to carve a space for future Anarchist activity and organizations." You don't have to be

Crazy Churches

St. Andrew Kim Korean Catholic Church

2108-2nd Ave. NW, 283-0933

Must be seen to be believed. Imagine a two-foot high bunker, sunk into a residential corner lot and surrounded by cheery flower beds. A short flight of wooden steps leads to a closet-sized "rooftop" shed. Visitors enter the shed and then immediately descend yet *another* flight of stairs into the bunker. Do you follow? In other words, you gotta go *up* to get *down*. (Gee, isn't that a James Brown song?) The end result looks like a giant submerged shoebox topped with two tiny birdhouses at opposite ends. (The second birdhouse is the church's backdoor. Safety first.)

The big question: Huh?

Some folks say the church burned to its foundation and the top-level was never rebuilt. But judging from the naked support stumps located around the bunker, the other much-bandied rumour seems more plausible: the congregation ran out of money during the building's construction, so they slapped a roof on their basement and called it a day.

Queen of Peace Church

2111 Uxbridge Dr. NW, 289-0111

M.B. Byrne's history of the Roman Catholic Diocese of Calgary, *From The Buffalo To The Cross*, simply calls the Queen of Peace Church "of an unusual design." Holy understatement! Instead of a traditional steeple, there's a huge, white, plastic-looking teepee rising out of the roof. "Unusual," yeah — but it's also pretty freakin' cool. Nice Pope bust out front, too.

---

a student to join. Club events include: overtaking the president's office (demands: no more student debt and ixnay on "corporate monopoly" dealings) and bringing mouthpieces like Jello Biafra to campus. They also play a lot of Risk.

Critical Mass

Adamantly *not* an organization, Critical Mass favours the coy designation of "unorganized coincidence." The idea for a spontaneous, monthly (pardon the inherent contradiction) gathering of cyclists originated in San Francisco circa 1992. Cyclists meet at a predetermined spot and then ride *en masse* through rush-hour traffic, literally taking their bikes-have-road-rights message to the streets. The Calgary Critical Mass "coincidentally" meets at the Hard Rock Café at 5:15 p.m. on the first Monday of the month. The route varies, but rides usually last 30 to 45 minutes.

Film/Video Societies

To quote Nellie McClung, "Never retreat, never explain, never apologize – get the thing done and let them howl." I'm not sure if she was talking about filmmaking, but it certainly sounds like good advice all the same. The following societies will help you "get the thing done." No guarantees on that howling stuff, though.

Calgary Society of Independent Filmmakers

500, 1304-4th St. SW, 205-4747

Formed in 1978, the Calgary Society of Independent Filmmakers is a non-profit society which encourages all aspects of indie filmmaking: production, exhibition, distribution, etc. The CSIF runs several workshops series, rents equipment and in-house editing/exhibition facilities, and offers a "Summer Media Arts Camp for Teens." The society also puts on the annual $100 Film Festival, which started in 1992 with seven Super-8 entries and just keeps getting bigger.

EM-Media

203, 351-11th Ave. SW, 263-2833

The "EM" stands for "media art," or something along those lines. At any rate, EM-Media (formerly Centre Art Video) is a media arts resource, production, and programming centre. In other words: workshops, presentations by visiting media artists, and so much, much more – all in the name of indie media art.

Quickdraw Animation Society

201, 351-11th Ave. SW, 261-5767

The Quickdraw Animation Society is a real Mickey Mouse operation. (Get it? Sorry.) The non-profit, artist-run film production co-op is dedicated to the production and appreciation of all forms and styles of animation: cel, puppet, clay, camera-less, painting on glass, backlit sand, etc. The QAS offers classes such as "Introduction to Classical 2D Animation" as well as courses for kids. Plus: animation workshops and free film nights.

Anti-Racist Action

Exactly what the name says. Write to the Calgary ARA at Box 23147, Connaught Postal Outlet, T2S 3B1.

Justabunchökids

Justabunchökids is a community-run collective dedicated to presenting affordable all-ages gigs. In addition to the music, the JBK maintain a crazy lending library that ranges from zines and Noam Chomsky books to communist tracts and *Hot Pantz: Do it Yourself Gynecology*. (To paraphrase Bill Cosby, kids can run the darndest collectives.) Justabunchökids share an office with Food Not Bombs in the Calgary Multicultural Centre (*712-5th St. SE, 266-8858*).

Maisons de Masons

Heirs to the ancient Knights Templar, determined to preserve a holy bloodline? An occult brotherhood whose membership gets all the best parking spots? Or benign average blokes who just happen to like fancy handshakes? Only the Freemasons themselves know the truth and they deny any role in covert world domination . . . but feigned innocence only makes them more suspicious, if you ask me.

To find out for yourself what those tricky rascals are up to, call the Masonic Hotline (275-0088) or drop by one of their six convenient locations and ask for the five-cent tour:

Grand Lodge (330-12th Ave. SW)
Ancient and Accepted Scottish Rite Lodge (so secret, they don't list the address)
Bowmont Masonic Lodge (7704-39th Ave. NW)
King George Masonic Lodge (223 Osborne Cres. SW)
St. Mark's Masonic Lodge (2612-14A St. SW)
Heritage Park Masonic Hall (not officially active, but Masons occasionally hang out there)

Hallowed Ground

The red brick building at 7248-25th St. SE holds many secrets, the least of which being its former life as an AGT substation. Years ago, Ratchadham Jetiyajarn (a Bangkok Buddhist master) handpicked Calgary for a retreat/meditation instruction centre devoted to Thai and Laotian followers. He selected the then-vacant substation to become his fourth Canadian temple. (On a geographic note, the temple is across the street from Fat Boy's Burgers. Insert Buddha joke here.) In 1998, the temple was the site of the first "Interment of the Nine Sacred Orbs" ceremony to be conducted in Western Canada. During the consecration ceremony, Buddhist monks buried eight large golden spheres in holes surrounding the building. A ninth orb was then suspended in the building's centre, thusly completing the ceremony and giving the temple the heavenly go-ahead to ordain monks.

Secret Town

Deep under the glacier-fed waters of Banff National Park's Lake Minnewanka lies the resort village of Minnewanka Landing, so named because it served as homebase for the original lake's many boat tours. In 1941, the town disappeared under the waves thanks to the latest in a succession of increasingly larger hydro-electric dams. Today, Lake Minnewanka is popular with scuba divers who explore the town's foundations, roads, bridges, and buildings. Some divers take a less-than-charitable approach to conservation: underwater vandalism ranges from run-of-the-mill graffiti to the rather imaginative act of bolting a toilet to the side of the lake's original wooden dam. (Yeah, yeah, it's irresponsible in that wrecks-things-for-everyone way, but come on – a toilet stuck to a dam is funny stuff any way you slice it.)

Eggheads Unite

Predating the Parisian "café philo" trend by a good five years, the Apeiron Society (est. 1987) meets in the Scandinavian Centre's basement *(739-20th Ave. NW)* every second Tuesday to wax philosophical. Each meeting is structured around a lecture on a sizzling topic such as "Diverse Readings: Philosophical & Political Implication Of Plato's Fictional Cities" or "Socrates In the Search Of Meaning: Towards A Transcendental Foundation." (Fret not, "Apeiron" may be Greek for "infinite" but the meetings only last a few hours.) The evening kicks off with the guest speaker, followed by coffee and a Q&A/squabbling session. The philosophical phestivities often continue over beer at Karouzos Pizza & Steak House. The Apeirons welcome average Joes, Josephines, and academics alike. Annual membership is $28, plus $3 per meeting. (Non-members can drop in for $6 a shot.)

Lest you think the Apeiron Society has cornered the café philo market: Annie's Book Co. *(912-16th Ave. NW)* holds evening meetings on the second Thursday of the month.

Some Great Reward

Union Cemetery's only remaining wooden headstone belongs to John Sibley. "Who was John Sibley?" you ask? I haven't the faintest. Time can be cruel, and if it weren't for the luck o' the draw, you wouldn't be reading the words "John Sibley " today. All that is known is he died on December 29, 1909 at the age of 10. On a lighter note, there's some sorta weird moss growing on his tombstone.

Everything's Preachy Keen

There's no local Scientology branch just yet — and I wouldn't touch 'em with a ten-foot pole (or five Tom Cruises stacked toe-to-head) if there was (they'd sue my pants off faster than I could say "Isaac Hayes hasn't made a good record since '73") — but there *are* plenty of other, shall we say, "alternative" churches to fill the void. Make of this information what you will.

**Calgary First
Spiritualist Church**
1603-6th Ave. NW, 283-1102

**The Spiritualist Society of the
Gateway Psychic Centre**
1609d Kensington Rd. NW, 270-3341
Spiritualism is "the science, philosophy, and religion of continuous life based upon the demonstrated fact of communication, by means of mediumship, with those who live in the Spirit World." In other words, pass the Ouija Board and don't fear the reaper.
Fun fact: In a weird way, grandpa really *is* "just taking a nap."
Turn-ons: Talking with the dead.
Turn-offs: Accidentally intercepting baby monitors.

War! Huh! Good god, y'all! What is it good for? It's good for a few laughs, I guess. Calgary is home to several commemorative troops of Riel Rebellion vintage (e.g. the Steele Scouts Frontier Society), but also a number of folks who cast their eyes even further back in history. In the mood for a historically-accurate playfight? You've come to the right place.

Medieval Arms Society of Calgary

Members painstakingly research medieval weapons and armour, then smack each other silly with full metal swordplay. That's right, *real* swords. *262-6220*

Musketeer Battle Club

"A social club for 17th Century enthusiasts." Members study various fencing techniques, as well as the proper way to wear a floppy hat (feather not included). *243-8662* (ask for Rob).

Society for Creative Anachronism

Much like the Medieval Arms Society, but using flat wooden swords. Babies.

Summer Street Festivals

Kensington Sun & Salsa Festival

The "sun" part is out of anyone's hands, but the "salsa" is guaranteed. This annual July festival (always a Sunday) finds Kensington businesses setting out their finest salsas, and passersby eating it all.

Lilac Festival

On the last Sunday in May, 4th St. SW is closed to traffic between 17th Ave. and Elbow Dr. Restaurants set up booths along the street, local musicians do their thing on various stages, and people pack the street like sardines. If it's a sunny day, forget about trying to do any of your usual 4th St. activities (like using a bank machine) and just go with the flow.

Marda Gras

No, it's not a typo. Marda Gras is Marda Loop's annual August street festival. For one Sunday out of the year, 33rd Ave. SW (from Crowchild Tr. to 19th St.) is closed to traffic and opened to live music, food, local artisans selling their wares, and if you're really lucky, pony rides.

Taste of Calgary

Held at Eau Claire Market in early August, Taste of Calgary is a festival of international food and drink. Various restaurants, breweries, etc. offer up tastes of what they do best (thus the catchy name). Your job, as a pedestrian, is to eat. Admission is free, but each sample (anything from turtle cakes to beer) will cost you a $1 token.

Church Universal and Triumphant

100, 1501-17 Ave. SW, 245-2467

Three cheers for Calgary, the Church Universal and Triumphant's Canadian HQ! Followers believe Elizabeth Clare Prophet, the CU&T's Alzheimer-addled leader, channels special spiritual messages from the "Ascended Masters." Founded in 1973, the American church gained notoriety in the '80s with the construction of numerous nuclear-proof bomb shelters. (Y'know, just in case.)

Fun fact: In 1997, a Cranbrook believer bought every single imported copy of the *Calgary Herald* to prevent locals from reading about the church's B.C. fallout shelter.

Turn-ons: All the Ascended Masters, including George Washington and Francis Bacon.

Turn-offs: Being called a cult.

Behind the Eightball

Scratch your itch to shoot some stick. On second thought, maybe "scratch" isn't the right word. Ah, you know what I mean.

Adams Family Billiard Arcade

781 Northmount Dr. NW, 282-1522

Black Wolf Billiards

4608 Macleod Tr. S, 287-2647

Chalk'n Rack Billiards & Family Amusements

1115 Falconridge Dr. NE, 285-6444

Diesel Billiards

1011-1st St. SW, 266-5116

Garage Billiards

Eau Claire Market, 262-6762

Great White Billiards

9, 6708 Macleod Tr. S, 253-1830

Haysboro Family Billiards & Arcade

9620 Elbow Dr. SW, 253-1668

Heritage Arcade & Billiards

220, 8220 Macleod Tr. S, 640-2560

Mike's Family Billiards Arcade & Pro Shop

34, 5010-4th St. NE, 274-0726

Olympic Billiards

1312-17th Ave. SW, 244-0606

Sunset Billiards & Arcade

1010-6th Ave. SW, 264-6499

Horse (Non)Sense

The St. Louis Hotel serves up 95¢ draft and greasy fried chicken every day of the week, but to catch "The World Famous Indoor Horseraces from East Calgary" you've gotta show up on Fridays for lunch. (Get there early, too. The place really fills up, especially during winter.)

Here's the deal: horseless horse-racing. For an hour (approx. noon 'til one) each Friday, George Stephenson grabs the mic and starts calling imaginary races. Armed only with the day's racing form (listing which fake horse is running in which fake race), George ad-libs his entire Kentucky Derby rap right on the spot. Yelling overtop a pre-recorded roar of hooves and horses, the 70-something retiree bounces up-and-down like an oversized jockey: "Air Fantasy is neck-and-neck with Windy Surf! Moonlight Martini is falling behind! And under the wire, it's...."

Patrons informally bet loonies amongst themselves, which makes for a good laugh at the finish line. Here's what always transpires: George yells out a horse's name ("Silver Chinook!") and whoever bet on said horse invariably emits a whoop of joy and starts raking up

Adios, Mortal Coil

We'll skip the whole "where does the spirit go?" navelgazing business and cut to the chase: when you die, you go into a hole in the ground. End of story. (Although there *are* some compelling arguments for taxidermy.)

Sometimes your final resting place may not be so final: the Chinese Cemetery, for example, was partially relocated in the '70s to accommodate the widening of Macleod Tr. But that's not the half of it: some people say a few unlucky, unmoved graves are now part of the roadway.

There are many factors when planning your big sleep, availability of space being one of them. Consumer note: avoid disappointment – don't delay, die today.

CITY-OWNED

Burnsland Cemetery
27th Ave. and Spiller Rd. SE
Full. Sorry.

Chinese Cemetery
Erlton St. and Macleod Tr. SW
Again, it's full. Keep looking.

Union Cemetery
27th Ave. and Spiller Rd. SE
Full. Looks like you're SOL once again.

St. Mary's Cemetery
Erlton St. and 32nd Ave. SW
Full, except for cremation.

Queens Park Cemetery and Mausoleum

32 Ave. and 4th St. NW

Jackpot! There's plenty of room at QP, which includes special Chinese, Jewish, and Catholic areas. Crypts, too.

OTHER

Eden Brook Memorial Gardens

*17th Ave. and
Lower Springbank Rd. SW*

Eden Brook is an all flat-bronze memorial cemetery. (That is, no upright monuments. Except for crypts.) In addition to the general plots (double- and single-depths available!), there's the Holy Family Catholic Cemetery and a Chinese area.

Mountain View Memorial Gardens

17th Ave. and Garden Rd. SE

Includes the Good Shepherd Catholic Cemetery, the Eternal Garden (Asian, including a special Buddhist area), and Resurrection Garden (Orthodox). Mountain View can handle the whole nine yards, from moment-of-death to burial.

Rocky View

911-32nd Ave. NE

The Rocky View Municipal District runs three separate rural resting places. Dalemead and Bottrel are both historical cemeteries (hundred-plus years old), located near tiny hamlets but still taking on new "guests." The larger Rocky View Garden of Peace offers Islamic, Chinese, and Catholic gardens, as well as the "mingled" multi-denominational area.

his/her winnings. Then George yells the name again ("Silver Chinook!"), followed by more cheers and the jingle of coins. Then the punchline: "Silver Chinook...is not the winner!" Groans fill the room. This goes on for a while, until George finally coughs up the real winner. Well, as "real" as an imaginary horse can be.

In between races (he calls four), George fills his time with Viagra jokes and shout-outs to various tables. The whole thing comes off like an hour of really whacked stand-up comedy, a stream of dirty jokes punctuated by bursts of Triple Crown Tourette's Syndrome. And did I mention the 95¢ beer?

Breakfast of Champions

Forget "retro," The National Hotel's coffee shop is authentic right down to the U-shaped arborite counters and torn vinyl seats. Sometimes the smells which escape the pull of the mighty stainless-steel fume hood are a little *too* authentic, if you know what I mean. But that's neither here nor there.

A quick scan of the plastic-lettered wall menu reveals few surprises (the usual greasy-spoon fare) until you hit the bottom: "Bill Collins Special $2." Two obvious questions jump to mind: (a) Who's Bill Collins? and (b) What's his special? Prepare for enlightenment.

Bill Collins is a retired steel mill worker and bronc-buster, a Saskatchewan transplant who visited the National many times as he worked his way across Western Canada. Always fond of the hotel, he's chosen it as his retirement home, and can be seen shuffling between the coffee shop, the tavern, and his room.

As for his special, it consists of two pancakes and two eggs. A man fond of life's simple pleasures, Bill Collins just puts margarine on his flapjacks. But the waitress says it's okay to put whatever you want on yours.

Media & Entertainment

Kurt Cobain slept here, but Cab Calloway didn't. Plus: cheap movies, Tommy Chong's paper route, Marilyn Monroe's ankle, the curse of *Superman III*, and a cast of thousands. Thousands of spiders, that is. Special bonus: not one, not two, but *three* Stooges.

Like a Canmore in the Wind

River of No Return (1954) was no cakewalk for Marilyn Monroe. Tension ran high on the set as director Otto Preminger and Marilyn's acting coach frequently knocked heads, and then Joe DiMaggio arrived unexpectedly to make sure co-star Robert Mitchum didn't get fresh with his bombshell wife. To top it all off, Marilyn's high-heel boots were no match for the Bow River's slippery rocks and she sprained her ankle something fierce. Marilyn's forest dressing room is no longer on its original spot, but a commemorative plaque marks the building's still-visible foundation. (At the risk of sounding redundant, the memorial can be found on the golf course side of Golf Course Road.)

Seven Inches Which Shook the World

It was the greatest publicity stunt since Mr. Carlson dropped all those turkeys from a helicopter on *WKRP*. In 1975, smalltime country singer and self-proclaimed "shit disturber" Cal Cavendish took to the sky in his single-engine plane. Cavendish buzzed the Calgary Tower (panicky diners were evacuated from the revolving restaurant) before unleashing 100 pounds of manure — and 100 copies of his "Government Issue" seven-inch single — over the downtown core. He was arrested, fined $3,000, and would've had his pilot's license revoked if he hadn't already lost it due to psychiatric reasons.

Cavendish is now a trucker specializing in, gulp, hazardous chemical transportation. (Relax, he's the proud recipient of a million-mile safe driving award.) He still sings his Stompin' Tom-ish tunes ("18 Wheeler Fever," "The Barf Bag Song") on occasion, and rented out the Jubilee Auditorium for a '94 comeback concert.

(Die-hard Caloholics are advised to check out *Cavendish Country*, a 1973 NFB short film.)

Here We Are Now, Entertain (all 253 of) Us

Nirvana's gig at the long-gone Westward Club *(119-12th Ave. SW, now just an empty room on the south side of the Holiday Inn)* is the Calgary indie-hipster equivalent of Woodstock: everyone says they were there and most of 'em weren't. (This was March 4th, 1991, just after Nirvana inked their deal with Geffen.) Kurt & Co. sang their happy songs for a full house, which by Westward standards was 253 people. For all you grunge historians, Attic Corrosion *(120-8th Ave. SW)* sells photocopied gig posters at $5 a pop. Cobain must be rolling in his grave. If he's really dead.

I'm Ready for my Yee-Haw, Mr. Demille

Calgary has been slowly building a reputation as "Hollywood North," not to be confused with those *other* Hollywood Norths like Vancouver or Yellowknife. When the cast 'n' crew of *Viper* (the latest in a long, distinguished line of television shows starring crimefighting cars — if you don't know, don't ask), rolled into town, industry insiders hoped the area's longstanding "wilderness" appeal was finally being replaced by "big city" razzmatazz. That said, a lot of the films and television series shot around these here parts still feature an inordinate amount of angry bears and/or pond hockey. Anyway, here's a selective list of Calgary's more notable screen appearances. (Geography sticklers be warned: I'm defining "Calgary" as pretty much anywhere above Montana and below Edmonton. So sorry.)

Shanghai Noon (filmed in 1999, unreleased at time of writing)
Far East meets Old West, under the loving gaze of wacky tough-guy Jackie Chan. (If you're still unclear on the concept, read the film's title out loud. Clever guy, that Jackie Chan.)

The Virginian (filmed in 1999, unreleased at time of writing)
Bill Pullman directs/stars in yet another movie based on some old television show. I call dibs on *B.J. & The Bear.*

Snow Day (filmed in 1999, unreleased at time of writing)
April's not a big snow month, even in Calgary. That's why 450 dumptruck loads of Canada Olympic Park's finest faux flakes were unloaded on Frontenac Avenue SW for this Chevy Chase comedy. Shirtless wonder Iggy Pop flew in to shoot a cameo.

Noah (1999)
Angered at the proliferation of poplar fluff floating around Elbow Park, Tony Danza reportedly threw a "hissy-fit" while filming this Bible-flavoured movie-of-the-week.

Mystery, Alaska (1999)
Russell Crowe cheesed the locals ("pulling a Danza" in filmspeak) when he started badmouthing hockey while drinking at Canmore's Drake

As a rah-rah leadup to the '88 Olympics, city hall ran a two-year "Song for Calgary" contest. The winning entry, "Neighbours of the World" by Victoria songwriters Tom Loney and Barry Bowman, was recorded by Kelita and Duncan Meiklejohn and released as a seven-inch single in March 1987. The song — how to put this delicately? — sucked. "Neighbours of the World" had that patented '80s "famine relief" sound (read: simultaneously uplifting and depressing) and vague lyrics reminiscent of those customized "your-child's-name-here" storybooks. (Honestly, what the heck does "You'll find your tomorrows here / You'll find it here today" mean? Does Calgary straddle some sort of international dateline the rest of us don't know about?) Local radio stations stopped playing the ditty within a week, and other cities ignored it entirely. CBS Records couldn't even give the thing away; after only a month, 7,500 souvenir records were gathering dust in a warehouse. A disc-jockey at AM-106 (now CKMX 1060) pulled no punches: "We actually got some people calling, asking us to never play it again. It was just the most dreadful song I've ever heard."

Photo: Courtesy of the CBC

On January 13, 1978, the CBC aired an afterschool nationalist potboiler called *Range Ryder & The Calgary Kid* in "The Adventure of the Dinosaur Badlands." The plot: a classic dressed-in-black bad guy declares himself Emperor of Alberta in a bid to sell the province to the States. His evil plot somehow involves taking an unwilling bride and blowing up a train carrying Wilfred Laurier. (As we all know, kids go wild for Canadian history.) But have no fear, Range Ryder and the Calgary Kid are here! The dynamic duo will stop at nothing to foil the dastardly scheme, even if it means riding tame dinosaurs. (Huh?) You simply *cannot* pack more action into 30 minutes.

Range Ryder was played by David Ferry, and a fourteen-year-old Mike Myers starred as the Calgary Kid. (Yeah, baby, *that* Mike Myers – that's him above, left.) Never one to leave any embarrassing rocks unturned, David Letterman enjoys tormenting Myers with this blast-from-the-past. Geographic footnote: *Range Ryder & The Calgary Kid* was filmed in the savage badlands of Toronto.

Radio Shack

Before founding CFCN, Bill Grant wet his radio-broadcasting feet with a 100-watt station called CHBC. The transmission tower was tucked away in the residential area of Rosedale, and the old CHBC shack-cum-studio can still be seen in the backyard of 708 Crescent Rd. NW. It's the small garage with the curved roof.

Inn. When an offended patron mentioned Crowe's inability to skate, the bad boy actor errupted into a glass-smashing, chair-throwing frenzy.

North of 60 (1992-1998)
The critically-acclaimed CBC television series about life in fictional Lynx River, N.W.T. was filmed west of Bragg Creek. Those in the abbreviation-friendly television biz simply call it "North Of."

The Jack Bull (1998)
While in town to film this bronc-bustin' HBO movie-of-the-week, John Cusack impressed the 17th Ave. crowd with his vast wardrobe of filthy clothes.

Wild America (1997)
J.T.T. (Jonathan Taylor Thomas for those of you who don't read *Tiger Beat*) tried to shuck his *Home Improvement* shackles with this coming-of-age road movie.

The Edge (1997)
Canmore residents knew this Mamet-scripted thriller by its working title (*Bookworm*) and its British star by

his nickname (Tony). Anthony Hopkins earned a good rep around town as a great hugger (honest) and excellent tipper. The film also stars Alec Baldwin and some bear. Check out the framed photos of Hopkins and Baldwin in Calgary's Rajdoot Restaurant *(2424-4th St. SW)*.

In Cold Blood (1996)
A small screen take on Truman Capote's new journalism classic, starring that guy from *ER*. Not George Clooney. The other guy.

How The West Was Fun (1994)
Alright already: Mary Kate and Ashley Olsen are identical twins. They look exactly alike. We *get* it. Now for the love of all that is holy, please stop.

Cool Runnings (1992)
The Jamaican Bobsled Team hadn't even seen snow before the '88 Olympics. This is their story. Starring John Candy.

Big McMistake

The Carthy Organ (housed in The Arts Centre's Jack Singer Concert Hall, 205-8th Ave. SE) is *waaaay* too big to be a secret. You can't very well overlook 6,040 pipes, especially when some of those things are 10 metres long. (If you laid all the pipes end-to-end, they'd span the English Channel.) But did you know the Carthy Organ was built in Québec, then dismantled and trucked to Calgary? Did you know there's a climate-controlled room beneath the concert hall which feeds the pipes with 62 cubic metres of wind per minute? My you're clever. Okay, did you know the $700,000 instrument was a gift from the super-wealthy, super-reclusive Mannix family? Knew that one too, huh? Alright wise guy, riddle me this: who the heck is Carthy anyway? The humble Mannix family doesn't toot its horn at the best of times, but they're especially mum about Carthy's identity. The tight lips are understandable: the organ was *supposed* to be named after Fred Stephen Mannix's great-grandmother, Elizabeth Mannix McCarthy – that's right, McCarthy – but a Mannix Foundation employee fumbled the name and it's been Carthy ever since. So there, smartypants.

Secret Sold-Out Seating

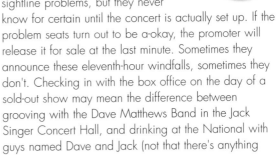

"Sold Out" doesn't have to mean "S.O.L." Concert halls regularly "kill" (i.e., don't sell) seats with *potential* sightline problems, but they never know for certain until the concert is actually set up. If the problem seats turn out to be a-okay, the promoter will release it for sale at the last minute. Sometimes they announce these eleventh-hour windfalls, sometimes they don't. Checking in with the box office on the day of a sold-out show may mean the difference between grooving with the Dave Matthews Band in the Jack Singer Concert Hall, and drinking at the National with guys named Dave and Jack (not that there's anything wrong with that).

The Stooges' Funhouse

Historically speaking, the Stampede has been graced by numerous distinguished visitors: Bob Hope, Jay "Tonto" Silverheels, Walt Disney, Robert F. Kennedy, the Queen of England. . . . But nothing, *nothing* can top July 1963, when three gentlemen named Moe, Curly, and Larry blew into town. For six days straight, twice a day (2:30 and 8:30 p.m.), the Stooges hammed it up at the Corral. Talk about the good ol' days: it makes contemporary Stampede entertainment fare seem — awww, who am I trying to kid? Impersonator Shania Twin is still awesome in every sense of the word. Nyuck, nyuck, nyuck.

Tragic and Hip

After they'd outgrown the tiny Westward Club, and before graduating to hockey arenas, the Tragically Hip enjoyed the middle ground that is the University of Calgary's MacEwan Hall Ballroom. (Other notable MacHall alumni include: R.E.M., Iggy Pop, and Vince Gill.) The Hip even used Ballroom concert footage in their "New Orleans Is Sinking" video, forever immortalizing the backs of many Calgarians' heads. Is that *your* sweat-soaked mullet bobbing in the mosh pit? Only your hairdresser knows for sure.

Unforgiven (1992)
Clint Eastwood's return to the western genre cinched both the Best Picture and Best Director Oscars.

Heaven & Earth (1991)
Ho hum. Yet another one of those $50M samurai epics.

Dead-Bang (1989)
Don Johnson's attempt to parlay *Miami Vice* stardom into big-screen success. *Nash Bridges*, anyone?

The Journey of Natty Gann (1985)
A Depression-era street urchin rides the rails from Chicago to Seattle, in search of her pa. With Meredith Salenger, John Cusack, and Scatman Crothers.

Superman III (1983)
You *will* believe a man can fly. Richard Pryor as a computer genius, however, is pushing it. By the way: Barons Consolidated School, a.k.a. "Smallville High" in the first two *Superman* movies, is in real-life danger of closing due to lack of kids. (But the school's rival institution, Lex Luthor Evil Academy and Finishing School, is doing just fine.)

Finders Keepers (1983)
Director Richard Lester (A Hard Day's Night, A Funny Thing Happened on the Way to the Forum) returned to his slapstick roots with this zany "chase" comedy. But any way you slice it, Lou Gossett Jr. and Beverly D'Angelo are poor replacements for Ringo Starr and Zero Mostel.

Death Hunt (1981)
Lee Marvin's mountie chased Charles Bronson's Mad Trapper all over Banff. Based on a true story.

Days of Heaven (1978)
Nowadays, writer-director Terrence Malick is a reclusive eccentric. We can say we knew him when. Malick celebrated this film's completion with a 20-year vacation.

Buffalo Bill & The Indians (1976)
Robert Altman directed Paul Newman, Joel Grey, and Harvey Keitel in this unhinged Western. Wry pop genius Randy Newman travelled to Calgary so he could hang around the set.

Kiss of the Spider Family

Marguerite and Stan Schultz began breeding tarantulas in their Michigan pet store during the '60s. Long since relocated to Calgary, the Schultzes share their NE home with the pitter-patter of up to 12,000 hairy legs. (Stan says the hobby is now "more of a psychosis" and is saddened to report that the spiders are restricted to one bedroom and a corner of the kitchen: "My wife put her foot down.") The couple are internationally-recognized tarantula experts and the authors of *The Tarantula Keeper's Guide*. They've even dipped their toe into showbiz; a tarantula named Tugboat Annie can be seen menacing miniature people in the *Honey, I Shrunk The Kids* television series. The Schultzes are happy to discuss their psychosis and might even give you a tour. Phone them at 230-1911. In case you're stuck for small talk, Stan also knows an awful lot about Renaissance-era pickled bugs.

The Bishop's Palace

Built in 1911, the house known as "The Bishop's Palace" *(910-7A St. NW)* was the kind of futuristic dwelling usually reserved for World's Fairs: a phone in every room, a built-in vacuum, and a fancy gizmo used to pump rooftop rainwater into the kitchen sink. (Sure it doesn't sound like much by today's standards, but this was hi-tech stuff in 1911.) The Roman Catholic church bought the house as a bishop's residence in 1918, hence the nickname. The mysterious Mannix Family now loans the Palace to the Calgary International Organ Festival, which uses the house as a residence for visiting musicians.

Anarchy in the NW

Don't ask me how it happened, but a palatial heritage home known as "The Manor" was ground zero for Calgary's early punk scene. Local scenesters and out-of-town bands alike crashed at this two-storey mansion, infamous for skateboard ramps and a soda-pop vending machine filled with beer. (Vintage Manor footage can be found in Social Distortion's *Another State of Mind* tour film, chronicling the SoCal band's hardluck life on the road. Mike Ness wrote the flick's title song while sitting on The Manor's front porch.) Somewhere along the line the punks got jobs and The Manor was moved into a nearby alley (one block east of the corner of 28th St. and 8th Ave. NW). The new owners have restored the house to its former glory, but neglected to relocate the heritage half-pipe.

Come Back to the Five & Dime, Tommy Chong, Tommy Chong

During the '50s, a young man named Tommy Chong delivered the *Calgary Herald* by day and played in a rock 'n' roll combo called The Shades by night. Fights often broke out during Shades gigs (they were *that* good), so then-mayor Don Mackay gave the boys the bum's rush in 1958. (The idea of being run out of town seems so Old West, but I guess you could still do such things in the '50s.) Chong headed to Vancouver, where he hooked up with a likeminded chap named Cheech Marin. After a disastrous stint as "Marin & Tommy," the duo changed their name and comedy history was born. And so, were it not for Calgary's anti-rock policy, the world may have never enjoyed classic Cheech & Chong routines such as "Dave's Not Here, Man" or that movie where they're both really stoned.

The Silver Streak (1976)
Yep, Richard Pryor again. This time he brought along soon-to-be *Stir Crazy* pal Gene Wilder.

Little Big Man (1970)
Alberta as the American Old West, and Dustin Hoffman as an 121-year-old man. Ah, the miracle of makeup.

Dr. Zhivago (1965)
So maybe it was only a few second unit scenery shots and it's not like Omar Sharif was scarfing teen-burgers at the Banff A&W. Forget I said anything.

Extra! Extra! Read All About Extras!

So you wanna work in the movie biz but Blockbuster isn't hiring? Consider working as an "extra." If you've got what it takes to portray "Woman On Bus #2" or "Guy In Cafe Wearing Sombrero and Silently Worrying About His Career," give the following agencies a whirl:

Nicki, Wild Dog of the North (1960) The Disney tale of a wild dog named Nicki and its fantastic adventures in the, er, north.

The Far Country (1955) James Stewart stars as a tough-as-nails cattleman trying to make a go of it during the Klondike gold rush. No imaginary rabbits or benevolent angels in this one, but it does co-star Harry "Col. Potter" Morgan.

Springtime in the Rockies (1942) Starring Betty Grable, John Payne, Cesar Romero, Jackie Gleason, Carmen Miranda, and a rising young starlet named Lake Louise. Songs, dance numbers, stunning scenery, and little-to-no plot.

Bette Chadwick, The Other Agency Casting Ltd.
266-6191

The Casting Line Canada Inc.
547-7398

Cinematic Casting
266-1918

Classic Casting
948-4563

Features
240-4468

Jarret Talent & Extras Management
590-2155

Power Film Extras
264-5997

Star Production Talent Agency
286-4577

Secret TV Channels

Everyone knows the higher you climb into the upper cable echelons, the greater the likelihood of cursing and nudity. It's one of life's great constants. But the truly discerning couch spud knows the *real* action is hidden in the cable stratosphere.

Featuring a 24-hour feed from various NASA projects (space shuttles, satellites), the late, lamented Channel 76 pumped out enough cloud cover to make a meteorologist blush. Sadly, all that's left of 76 is muzak-jazz and a looped message vaguely explaining the channel's absence. Did someone say "cover-up"?

Equally suspicious is Ch. 78, a blurry line graph accompanied by cryptic notation. The line goes up, the line goes down – but what does it all mean? Someone's hospital life support, mistakenly leaked to the airwaves? Plate-shifting Richter rumblings beneath our fair city? Should we panic, or just surf over to *Ally McBeal*?

A quick call to Shaw Cable alleviated any fears regarding the mysterious Ch. 78. "That's just a testing channel for our cable signal," explained a helpful chap. He assured me it's of no concern to viewers if the graph happens to, say, flatline at 2 a.m. And the whole deal has buppkiss to do with earthquakes. Or so they say.

Secret Broadcast Booth

Long plagued by financial woes (it was even declared DOA for a brief period not so long ago), CKUA somehow always manages to keep on truckin'. The province-wide FM station broadcasts from Edmonton, but it also maintains a small broadcast booth in Calgary. Located in a converted coat-check in the upper lobby of The Arts Centre's Jack Singer Concert Hall, CKUA South is the source of news broadcasts, a pre-recorded First Nations music/culture/issues program (*First Voices*, Thursday evenings, 8:30-9), and the live-to-air *Deuces Wild* (Saturday mornings, 9-11). Special bonus: you can stare at the DJs from the Plus-15, which I'm sure they enjoy immeasurably.

Cinema de Skinflint

On one hand, it's a depressing sign of the times: behemoths like the Famous Players Coliseum are squeezing smaller theatres into second-run discount purgatory. On the other hand, it sure is easy on the consumer's billfold. Besides, watching a Christmas comedy in July is good for the spirit.

Moviedome (Franklin Mall)
3516-8th Ave. NE, 248-2000
$2.50 weeknights, $2 matinees, $1 all day Tuesday

Northland Village
5111 Northland Dr. NW, 288-9141
$2.50 all the time

Showcase Grand
608-1st St. SW, 264-1700
$6 weeknights, $4 Tuesdays
(Note: higher prices, but more current movies. And it's easily the coolest theatre in the city.)

Southland
Macleod Tr. and Southland Dr. SW, 255-2175
$2.50 all the time

GO DOG GO

Music-video director Jeth Weinrich has worked with superstars like Van Halen, Jann Arden, and Anne Murray. His mom's Calgary clothing store (*Sagesse, 801-17th Ave. SW*) is a veritable shrine to Weinrich's achievements; stop by and check out the wall o' awards. But his biggest claim to fame is losing his dog. Weinrich left his dog (Bill) outside an HMV during a 1998 visit to New York City. A security guard spooked the 11-year-old Australian blue heeler, who booted into Central Park and eventually made his way into the Holland Tunnel. Then Bill vanished.

Weinrich spent $10,000 on newspaper ads and offered a $5,000 reward for the dog's return. Days later, a car struck Bill as he tried to cross four lanes of the New Jersey Turnpike. A good Samaritan rescued the injured pup, and a happy Weinrich was reunited with his doggy pal. All the hubbub landed the duo on *Late Night with Conan O'Brien, Rosie O'Donnell, Hard Copy, Inside Edition,* and *Dateline.*

Footnote: Bill is no stranger to mischief. During the filming of 54•40's "Ocean Pearl" video, the kooky canine hopped into an empty vehicle, pawed the locks shut, and promptly fell asleep. The problem: it was high noon in the middle of the Arizona desert, and Bill chose to commandeer the only air-conditioned place on the entire set. He was not a popular dog that day.

The Great Escapism

Pilot Officer Barry Davidson was one of five Calgary brothers who saw active service during WWII. His first (and only) European mission was shortlived: en route to bomb a Parisian aerodome, Davidson crashed his Blenheim bomber in German-occupied territory. The 26-year-old flyboy spent the next two years imprisoned in Stalag Luft I, where he constructed makeshift sports equipment for fellow hockey-starved inmates. Transferred to Stalag Luft III, Davidson – or, as he came to be known around the camp, "The Scrounger" – used his pick-a-part skills to scavenge materials for a year-long escape-tunnel excavation – a scheme later immortalized on the silver screen as *The Great Escape.* Davidson returned to live in Calgary after the war. He travelled to Toronto for the 1963 Canadian premiere of *The Great Escape,* starring James Garner as The Scrounger. Typical of the film's Hollywood revisionism, Scrounger was reworked as an American. Davidson thought the flick was "a lot of B.S."

No Animals Were Hurt in the Filming of this... Uh, Forget It

Contrary to popular belief, lemmings do not commit mass suicide by stampeding over cliffs and into the sea. 'Tis simply untrue. This delightful bit of misinformation was spread by none other than Walt Disney in his 1958 nature "documentary" *White Wilderness.* The film was shot in Alberta, despite the area's complete lack of (a) lemmings and (b) ocean. The filmmakers imported lemmings from Manitoba and faked up "suicidal migration" footage by herding the critters off a cliff, recording their unhappy plummet into an awaiting river. Details are understandably sketchy regarding this shameful bit of cinematic history, so it's unclear as to exactly *where* in Alberta this fiasco occurred. Given the area's abundance of buffalo jumps, however, Calgary is a darn good bet.

Superstitious film buffs believe *Rebel Without a Cause* (1955) to be "cursed" because its three hot young stars (James Dean, Natalie Wood, Sal Mineo) all met violent, untimely deaths. (Granted, the 26-year spread between Dean and Wood's respective passings makes the whole "curse" biz more than a little dubious.) That said, the filmed-in-Calgary *Superman III* (1983) has its own suspicious history. Not only is *Superman III* widely-regarded as the crummiest of the supermovies, but three of its four stars have fallen on hard times. In fact, Christopher Reeve (Clark Kent/Superman) literally fell on hard ground when he was bucked from a horse in 1995. His neck broken, Reeve is now famously confined to a wheelchair. In 1996, Margot Kidder (Lois Lane) flipped out in Los Angeles: she hacked off her hair, swapped clothes with a derelict, somehow lost her false teeth, and was eventually discovered sleeping in an unsuspecting family's backyard leaf pile. (But she's feeling *muuuuuch* better now.) Unlucky #3 is Richard Pryor (Gus Gorman), his body now ravaged by multiple sclerosis. You may remember the scene in which Pryor's pink-afghan-clad character literally stops traffic by skiing off Esso Plaza, landing smackdab in the middle of 6th Ave.

A curse? Maybe it's simple coincidence, but even hardened disbelievers gotta admit it's kind of freaky. Robert Vaughn (*Superman III*'s evil villain) must be shaking in his boots.

GUNS, CARS, AND SITARS

Nicknamed "Ballywood" because of its staggering rate of output, India's film scene is big business. Local rep-cinema war-horse The Plaza *(1133 Kensington Rd. NW)* has been Calgary's Ballywood connection since the '70s, screening the flicks during weekend matinees and Friday/Saturday late shows. The super-popular films are famous for their surreal juxtaposition of fighting, dancing, and singing (the latest addition to the action: kissing), meaning Western audiences should be able to follow along just fine without subtitles. (Pea-sized bladder

How Gangrene was My Valley

The human half of a trained goat act, W.B. Sherman moved to Calgary after his garbage-eating partner died. (Don't ask.) The flamboyant entrepreneur bought the Hull Opera House in 1905, renaming it the W.B. Sherman Opera House. He also owned a theatre troupe (The Sherman & Summer's Stock Company) and an ice rink (The Sherman Ice Skating Rink). Are you picking up a pattern here?

All that remains of the Sherman empire is the Showcase Grand cinema *(608-1st St. SW)*, formerly the (what else?) Sherman Grand. Back then the theatre presented vaudevillian entertainment, hosting performers such as the Marx Brothers and a 12-year-old kid named Fred Astaire. Today, the building is in danger of demolition, and preservationists are quick to brag about another Grand guest: Sarah Bernhardt.

Everything's "Sarah Bernhardt *this*" and "Sarah Bernhardt *that*," but the real scoop ain't so divine. The 69-year-old dame made her sole Calgary appearance in 1913. Sporting a gangrenous leg destined for amputation, Bernhardt sat in a chair while performing excerpts from *Camille* and *Lucretia Borgia*. She wasn't much better offstage. Oblivious to being in McClung territory, Bernhardt lambasted the suffragette movement as "a mistake."

"Men are the natural leaders and lawmakers," argued the Divine Miss Limpy, "and it is the height of folly for women to attempt to aspire to such positions."

This is the stuff of legends? Then again, maybe it was just her rotting limb talking.

alert: the movies often run for more than three hours, but there is an intermission.) The Ballywood bootlegging scene is extremely speedy (bootleg videos hit the streets within days of a film's theatrical release), forcing legit distributors to aim for simultaneous global premieres. In other words, Calgarians get to see latest sing/fight/sing epic at virtually the same time as Delhi or Bombay audiences. Plaza fans who are suffering weekday Ballywood withdrawal are advised to check out the Franklin Mall Moviedome, which has recently begun showing the flicks Monday to Thursday.

Photo: Sven Schwirin

Looking back, it was only a matter of time before Michael Moriarty set his sights on Calgary. Any place capable of spawning both Ralphie *and* the Amazing Presto must look mighty inviting to a delusional egomaniac giddy with visions of political greatness. A highly-regarded actor and composer, Moriarty left his comfy U.S. existence (success, marriage, *Law and Order*) for the refuge of Nova Scotia. After gaining a lot of weight ("I like my girth"), and losing both his sanity and a Halifax barfight, the self-styled Churchillean figure made known his plans to one day assume Calgary's mayoral throne. (It's all part of his bigger Republican Party of Canada scheme, his "one-man war against the federal government," but why Calgary? Guess his 1999 gig with the CPO made a favourable impression on the nut.) Calgarians received a taste of things to come when Moriarty and *Herald* columnist Catherine Ford traded barbs in a pissy he-said/she-said exchange. She said it didn't sound "like all of your lumber has been loaded into the truck bed," he called her "too polite and too condescending for me to determine anything except your profound complacence." (He went on to call *himself* "one of the three great alcoholics of the 20th century," but that's beside the point.) And so the dance begins.

film festivals

A certain local television station used to show, like, all the *Planet of the Apes* movies back-to-back through the wee hours. But that was during simpler times, long before the powers-that-be succumbed to the irresistible lure of infomercial bucks. Sigh. I miss Dr. Zaius. On a brighter note, there are other boss film festivals to keep your head occupied:

Fairy Tales: A Gay and Lesbian Film and Video Festival

June 1999 was the first year for this Calgary Society of Independent Filmmakers/Gay and Lesbian Community Services Association co-production. Will they do it again? Who the hell knows.

HERLAND: Feminist Film and Video Celebration

Held in late winter/early spring, Calgary's annual femme-festival is only one of two in Canada. The other's in Newfoundland, just so you know.

The $100 Film Festival

Like a toddler fortified with Flintstones chewable vitamins, this festival just keeps getting bigger every year. Entries are no longer restricted to a hundred-smacker budget, but the emphasis is still on low-low-low shoestring shorts. Presented by the Calgary Society of Independent Filmmakers, every November.

old school cinemas

There's not a lot of 'em, but Calgary has a few trusty alternatives to the Hollywood money machine.

The Globe Cinema

617-8th Ave. SW, 262-3308
The selections can be a touch on the mainstream side, but there's usually something worth checking out on either of The Globe's two screens.

The Plaza Theatre

1133 Kensington Rd. NW, 283-3636
The city's longest-running rep-house brings in everything from the straight-up (*Shakespeare In Love*) to the freaky (*Tribulation 99*). One screen, but generally quick turnover.

The Uptown Stage and Screen

612-8th Ave. SW, 265-0120
The owners swear on a stack of *Film Comments* that The Uptown will rise again. Until said time, it's only open for occasional (very, *very* occasional) events.

The Cotton Club it Ain't

Cab Calloway was booked to play a three-week stint at the old Sheraton Hotel (*202-4th Ave. SW,* now the International) in March 1976. Trouble was, the 69-year-old scat legend and self-styled "reefer man" was stuck with a hastily assembled back-up band. Calloway played one show, found the local musicians not up to snuff, and was in an airport-bound taxi faster than you can say "hi-de-ho." Total time spent in Calgary: 12 hours.

Honey I Shrunk the Special Effects Budget

The hopelessly starstruck are advised to hotfoot it down to the Inglewood Mr. Wrought Iron (*9th Ave. SE*), where you can have your picture snapped with oversized flowers built for the *Honey, I Shrunk The Kids* television series. Staff will happily take your photo, as long as you're willing to wait a week or two for final product. Pretend you're miniscule! Pretend you're in danger of being eaten by a giant cat! Pretend that guy from *Bosom Buddies* is your dad! Warning: the flowers still get hauled to the set on occasion, so they're not always there. Guard against disappointment accordingly.

Nighttime is the right time for live talk shows, drunken poets, freaky cabarets, and thou. Throw a *nouveau* cocktail (or two) into the mix, and we're talking a rip-snortin' good time. (Karaoke, you say? Let's not get crazy.) Gee whiz, that old song was right all along: after midnight, you really *can* let it all hang out.

Hotnuts and Popcorn

On Fridays at 11 p.m., a handful of Loose Moose alums throw together an untelevised late-night talk show that's somewhere between Jay Leno and Larry Sanders. The action happens in the Moose's Garry Theatre, where the host and sidekick – named, yep, Hotnuts and Popcorn (but nobody will say who's who) – are joined by a low budget "orchestra" and a sassy headbanger technician. Yeah, there's guests (like local kiddie television legend Buckshot), but when you've got a guy sporting feathered hair and a cut-off T-shirt working the lights, that's all the entertainment you could possibly need. Added bonus: the audience is encouraged to "come drunk."

Fashion Victim

Sure it's elegant *now*, but. . . . Beginning in the late 1950s, the Palliser Hotel was given a series of trendy makeovers best reserved for suburban rumpus rooms. (Shag carpet, anyone?) During the '60s, the Oak Room spent an unfortunate spell as "The Big Top Lounge," complete with carnival tent roof, revolving chandelier, and suspended merry-go-round horses. It is unclear whether would-be patrons had to meet a height requirement.

Photo: Courtesy of the Palliser Hotel

Hail Caesar, Full of Clams

Many people erroneously believe the Caesar (1 ounce vodka, 4 ounces tomato-clam juice, a dash of Worcestershire sauce, and a splash or two of horseradish) was invented at Caesar's Steakhouse. That would be too easy. The delightful potion was in fact born at the Calgary Westin Hotel. In 1969, the owners asked Walter Chell, the hotel's bar manager, to whip something up for their new Italian restaurant. Thinking something along the lines of "Clams and tomatoes taste great on pasta so why not mashed together in a glass?" Chell spent three months perfecting his fresh clam "nectar." And so history was made.

Note: it would be three years before Duffy Mott of California would invent the labour-saving Clamato juice. May the miracles of the modern world never cease.

Mountain City Madness

Bored with city nightlife? Head for the hills. *Rolling Stone* gave Banff top marks for spring skiing and being "the STD capital of Canada." (Hold on a minute! Is it true about the skiing?) The Banff Rose & Crown was also voted best place "to watch a good fight break out." Dude!

Secret Drinking Club

Time was you had to be a serviceman (or at least have one in the immediate family tree) to drink at the Legion. Now, thanks to an aging/declining membership, the RCL has instituted "fraternal, non-voting" status for the Average Joe. Any ol' Canadian citizen can now waltz in off the street and fill out an application. If the Legion's high mucka-mucks approve the application, one need only cough up the annual dues and you're eligible to be sworn in at the next available monthly meeting. Dues vary from Legion to Legion; the Bowness Branch No. 238, for e.g., charges $31 a year. (Note: it takes a while for official membership cards to arrive from Ottawa, so newcomers are given a temporary receipt-of-payment to flash at the door.) At ease, soldier.

Shaken, Stirred, Spilled Down My New Shirt

No city with a brewery as good as Big Rock will ever entirely forsake beer, but the cocktail revolution is definitely in full swing. If nothing else, it's sweet relief to finally see bars that aren't: (a) neon shrines to American bilgewater, or (b) *faux* pubs that are about as British as Grandpa Gunther's lederhosen. (Note to all bar owners: your fine establishment does not fall under either of the above categories, making you still eligible to spot me a few rounds until payday. Just so there are no misunderstandings.)

Some fine *nouveau* cocktail establishments:

The Mercury
801B-17th Ave. SW, 541-1175
The Mercury kickstarted the Calgary cocktail revival a few years back with its dark wood and boxing decor. Still cool, but now it can get kinda . . . uh, loud.

Concorde
510-17th Ave. SW, 228-4757
Straight outta the pages of *Wallpaper**, this Starckian restaurant/club serves up rum and

Cubasian cuisine. (Sadly, the jellyfish fishtank has been discontinued due to leakage.) Thursday night features the power-soul of Yomozo.

The Belvedere

107-8th Ave. SW, 265-9595

Sip a martini in the lounge and pretend you can afford dinner in the restaurant.

Ming

520-17th Ave. SW, 229-1986

Chairman Mao smiles down from above the fireplace, giving a Commie thumbs-up to this weird basement space. Generous use of naughahyde and a Cold War theme (not to mention ace sandwiches) make Ming a swell hideout — if you get there before the crowds make it a zoo.

Criterion

121-8th Ave. SW, 232-8080

Home to the grooviest wall in the city (must be seen, too hard to explain) and a semi-coed washroom (not quite *Ally McBeal* territory, but close). Bonus: within stumbling distance of the city's finest head shoppes.

The Cocktail Club

1530-5th St. SW, 228-1621

Surely I jest.

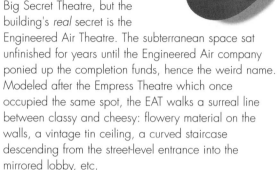

Secret Theatre

One Yellow Rabbit may bill their Arts Centre headquarters as the Big Secret Theatre, but the building's *real* secret is the Engineered Air Theatre. The subterranean space sat unfinished for years until the Engineered Air company ponied up the completion funds, hence the weird name. Modeled after the Empress Theatre which once occupied the same spot, the EAT walks a surreal line between classy and cheesy: flowery material on the walls, a vintage tin ceiling, a curved staircase descending from the street-level entrance into the mirrored lobby, etc.

In addition to various community programming, the EAT is home to two stellar annual music series: The Engineered Air Theatre Songwriters Series (past performers include Chip "Wild Thing" Taylor, Anne Loree, and Steve Forbert) and The Carma Unplugged Blues Series (John Hammond, Alvin Youngblood Hart, Kelly Joe Phelps). Believe you me, nuthin' sounds so sweet as slide guitar bouncing off brass.

Rub-A-Dub-Dub, Several Men in a Tub

The building occupying the NW corner of the 17th Ave./2nd St. SW intersection is the former headquarters of the long-gone Model Milk Company. (You can still see the carved milk jug cornerstones near the roof.) It's been long rumoured that the old dairy facilities stretch underneath 17th Ave. and butt up against (no pun intended) the funeral home across the street. Adding zest to this urban myth is the fact that the Model Milk basement houses Goliath's Sauna (229-0911), a gay bathhouse. A lot of people really like the idea of naughtiness beneath the asphalt, but Goliath's insists they only occupy a level-and-a-half of regular ol' basement. One thing's for sure: Goliath's is open 24-7, giving new meaning to the phrase "rubber ducky, you make bath-time lots of fun."

What follows is a highly arbitrary cross-section of watering holes. Some offer live music, some DJs, and others little more than a tall cool one. Clubs open and close in the blink of an eye, so who knows what the city will look like in six months. For now, consider this a snapshot:

The Auburn Saloon
712-1st St. SE
Close proximity to The Arts Centre makes the Auburn a popular post-theatre watering hole for artists and audiences alike. Girlie-drink enthus-iasts simply *must* try a "Johnny R."

The Back Alley
4630 Macleod Tr. S
The only place to hear live death metal on a regular basis. Plus: a who's-huh? of where-are-they-now rockers still slugging it out on the road (Chilliwack, Headpins, etc.).

The Back Lot
209-10th Ave. SW
Gays! Lesbians! Martinis!

Beat Niq Jazz and Social Club
811-1st St. SW
Super-cool live jazz room hidden underneath the Piq Niq Cafe. Très New York.

Boystown/The Rek Room
213-10th Ave. SW
Members-only club, for the quintessential guy's guy.

Capital
105, 401-9th Ave. SW
Various DJs spin R&B, soul, funk, Latin, world beat. . . .

Castle Pub
1217-1st St. SW
You know you're a bike courier when. . . .

Detour
318-17th Ave. SW
Gay/lesbian dance bar. Thursdays are women only, Fridays are for men. Sunday, however, belongs to the drag queens.

Nocturnal Mastication

It's late. Maybe you're drunk. The call of the wild is crying out to you: eat as much fat as possible, and quickly. Other than a Mac's heat 'n' eat sub, or one of the omnipresent 24-hour Denny's (six locations scattered throughout the city), here are a few wee-hour suggestions:

Blackfoot Truck Stop
1840-9th Ave. SE, 269-1636
A great place to practice your *Convoy* lingo. (Trust me, long-haul truckers just *love* hearing that sorta thing from drunkards. 10-4, good buddy.) Open 24 hrs.

Golden Inn
107A-2nd Ave. SE, 269-2211
Cantonese cuisine in the heart of Chinatown. Open 'til 2:30 a.m. Sunday to Thursday, and 3:30 a.m. on Friday and Saturday.

Harbour City Restaurant
302 Centre St. S, 269-8888
It's too late for the dim sum, but you can still load up on Peking and Cantonese delights. Open 'til 2 a.m. Sunday to Thursday, and 4 a.m. on Friday and Saturday.

The Homestead Restaurant & Pizza Place

1410-17th Ave. SW, 245-0555

You can get gravy on pretty much anything at the Homestead. (Probably even the pizza, if you're polite enough.) Depending on how much you've had to drink, you may not be able to lift the cast iron chairs. Open 'til 2:30 a.m. Sunday to Thursday, and 4 a.m. on Friday and Saturday.

Husky House

1201-5th St. SW, 237-7789

If it's good enough for the boys in blue, it's good enough for you. Open 24 hours.

Manie's Pizza

509-19th Ave. SW, 228-9207

When a single slice simply won't do, you can always party with Manie. Open 'til 5 a.m. every day.

Pongo

524-17th Ave. SW, 209-1073

Noodles, tiny televisions playing silent Kung Fu flicks, and maybe a DJ. Open 'til 2 a.m. Sunday to Thursday, and 4:30 a.m. on Friday and Saturday.

Ducky's Pub
5, 2100-4th St. SW

The kinda homey place where irate patrons stalk into the DJ booth and turn off the music. All that, plus billiards, close-captioned television, and karaoke.

Dusty's Saloon
1088 Olympic Way SE

"Dusty" in both name and housekeeping. A great selection of draught beer. (You do like Molson Canadian, right?)

The Embassy
516C-9th Ave. SW

Three floors of non-stop dance insanity and DJs galore.

James Joyce Pub
114 Stephen Ave. Walk SW

Irish to the point of offering Guinness in your choice of three temperatures, even though most people can't tell the diff. The Celtic stylings of Clanterra are "in the house" every Wednesday. Bonus: some rooms feature doctored photos of Jimmy J. hobnobbing with the pub's owner. (She's the one sans eyepatch.)

Java Sharks
529-17th Ave. SW

College-rock competition for the neighboring Ship & Anchor. Lots of live music, including regular Battles of the Bands. Open-mic poetry, too.

Kaos Jazz Bar and Bistro
718-17th Ave. SW

Recently renovated, the Kaos features the bluesy likes of Dutch Mason, Tim Williams, and Lester Quitzau.

Karma Local Arts House
2139-33rd Ave. SW

Live acoustic, original music seven nights a week. Karma runs a "Songwriters in the Round" concert series on Sunday nights, which attracts the likes of Ian Tyson and Big Dave McLean.

Money Pennies Restaurant and Bar
111-15th Ave. SW

Gay/lesbian bar. Live entertainment, reading nook, patio, etc.

The Nash
1042-10th Ave. SE

Back when it was just the plain ol' "National Hotel," this was Calgary's main punk/alternative club. (Lots of people like to believe a trio of bottle-blonde unknowns called The Police played here to a handful of uninterested patrons. They didn't. But 54•40 did.) These days, The Nash offers live music (mostly blues) seven nights a week. Kelly Jay, of Crowbar fame, hosts the weekend jams.

The Newt
107-10A St. NW

Odd, multi-level establishment. Features beer all the time, comedy some of the time.

Orbit
221-17th Ave. SW

A regular cast of DJs spin jungle, drum & bass, and the entire "house" family.

The Palace
219 Stephen Ave. Walk SW

Freshly-renovated old movie theatre now gives Cowboys and The Back Alley a run for the cream of the washed-up rock circuit (Men at Work, Platinum Blonde, et al). The club also embraces the swing revival with the kind of enthusiasm once reserved for line-dancing.

Quincy's
609-7th Ave. SW

The building formerly known as Lucifer's has come long way since the hair-metal years. A snazzy establishment, Quincy's offers live music (jazz, songwriters), and is a favourite haunt of local lounge royalty The Dino Martinis.

The Republik
219-17th Ave. SW

Longstanding "alternative" music bar has welcomed everyone from Robyn Hitchcock to Oranj Symphonette to Bran Van 3000. Currently enjoying a weird DJ and geriatric punk (Mix Master Mike, U.K. Subs) phase.

Rooks Bar and Beanery
112-16th Ave. NW

A sports bar for women who love hockey and the women who love them. If you know what I'm sayin'. But men are welcome.

Wicked Wedge Pizza Co.
618-17th Ave. SW, 228-1024
More expensive than the various $2/slice pizza shacks, but far superior pie. Open 'til 1 a.m. Monday to Wednesday, and 3 a.m. Thursday to Saturday.

Karaoke and Name-That-Tune

Here's a little story for ya. A certain rough 'n' tumble bar is legendary for its karaoke nights, a magical time when the apes sing like angels. A good time is guaranteed as long as everyone adheres to one simple rule: "My Way" is off-limits. By order of management, only one person (we'll call him "Bill") can touch the song. It's said that when "Bill "takes the mike, the owner pauses whatever he's doing to listen in silent, misty wonder.

The following list of karaoke joints is by no means complete, but it should help you scratch your itch to warble "House of the Rising Sun." Added bonus: karaoke's kissin' cousin, the increasingly-popular Name-That-Tune.

Buffalo Bob's
126, 3715-51st St. SW, 686-1404
Name-That-Tune: Saturdays

Schanks Athletic Club

9627 Macleod Tr. S
103 Crowfoot Terr. NW

"Sports bars" in the most literal sense: bowling alleys, beach volleyball, virtual golf, mini-golf, and booze. Warning: don't drink and putt.

Ship & Anchor

534-17th Ave. SW

A weird mix of traditional British pub trappings (World Cup soccer on the tube, dusty books on the shelves) and alt-rock music. In addition to frequent nighttime rock gigs, the Ship holds afternoon open-stages every Saturday. Their annual Patsy Cline/Hank Williams tribute night is a Stampede tradition.

Swans

1336-9th Ave. SE

Cozy Inglewood pub features the bizarre game known as Naglan: two opponents race to hammer nails into a stump . . . using the claw end of a hammer. Don't ask.

Tullamore

Upstairs, 124-10th St. NW

Easy-to-miss (look up, look waaay up) Irish pub serves up great food/beer in quaint environs. Nice patio.

The Underground Pub

731-10th Ave. SW (downstairs)

It came from beneath The Warehouse: "Trailer Park Tuesdays" (DJs spinning everything from honkytonk to industrial), and a whole lotta alt-rock.

The Warehouse

731-10th Ave. SW

Private club for members and guests. DJs serve up BritPop, house, industrial, and the like. Also hosts Goth nights every now and then.

Ducky's Pub

5, 2100-4th St. SW, 245-6585

Karaoke: Thursdays, Fridays, Saturdays

Hannibal's Pub

708-16th Ave. NW, 284-2291

Karaoke: Wednesdays, Fridays, Saturdays

Name-That-Tune: Mondays

Mike's Pizza and Cozy Pub

918-12th Ave. SW, 245-4646

Karaoke: Thursdays

New Dynasty Restaurant

601-17th Ave. SW, 245-2825

Karaoke: Fridays

Point and Feather

735 Ranchlands Blvd. NW, 241-2877

Name-That-Tune: Fridays

Stavro's Pizza and Sports Bar

4105-4th St. NW, 284-4504

Name-That-Tune: Saturdays

Wolfman's Pub

2118-33rd Ave. SW, 246-0778

Karaoke: Wednesdays, Thursdays

Name-That-Tune: Tuesdays (but for legal reasons they call it "Pubapalooza")

The King Edward Hotel (*438-9th Ave. SE*) calls itself "the home of the blues." The photos lining the nic-stained walls back up the boast: Sonny Rhodes, Paul Butterfield, Eddie Shaw, Legendary Blues Band, Koko Taylor, Otis Rush, Clarence "Gatemouth" Brown, Buckwheat Zydeco, Buddy Guy, Junior Wells, Luther "Guitar Junior" Johnson, Pinetop Perkins, Duke Robillard, Robert Jr. Lockwood. . . .

Built in the early 1900s, the Eddy has seen various rough 'n' tumble incarnations over the years (including a stint as a biker bar), but twenty years in the blues biz have earned the place a worldwide rep. In addition to its live-blues-every-night policy, The Eddy runs a summer blues festival which brings in talent such as neo-traditionalist Delta *wunderkind* Alvin Youngblood Hart. All that, plus the longtime Saturday afternoon/Sunday evening jam sessions (hosted by local legend Bill Dowey and his Blues Devils) which attracts everyone from basement hobbyists to John Hammond.

Drunken Poets Society

The brainchild of Sheri-D Wilson, Fred Hollis, and Kirk Miles, the Drunken Poets Society convenes every Monday night at 9:30 in the east wing of the Ship & Anchor. Topics include: poetry, drinking. In addition to the regular crew, the occasional out-of-town poet has been known to drop by for a pint. Poetry is read, beer is downed, and a good time is had by all. (Secret tip: if you show up and can't figure out which table is the DPS meeting, loudly announce "Anyone in here own a purple Valiant parked in front of a fire hydrant?" Works every time.)

Brew Pubs

Anyone can pop a bottle-cap or tap a keg, but it takes a real Martha Stewart kinda go-getter to actually brew his/her own beer. Brew pubs aren't a huge thing in Big Rock City, but two mainstays (and one in Canmore) have carved a niche for themselves:

Brewsters Brewing Company & Restaurant
834-11th Ave. SW, 265-2739
176, 755 Lake Bonavista Dr. SE, 225-2739
25 Crowfoot Terrace NW, 208-2739
Number of different beers: twelve
Biggest sellers: Hammerhead Red Ale, Flying Frog Lager, Wild West Wheat Ale

The Grizzly Paw Pub & Brewing Company
622-8th St., Canmore, 678-9983
The Rockies' only brew pub.
Number of different beers: six (five core, one rotating)
Biggest sellers: Grumpy Bear Honey Wheat Ale (Gold Medal winner at the 1999 Brewtopia festival), Drooling Moose Pilsner, Beaver Tail Raspberry Ale

Wildwood Brewing Company

2417-4th St. SW, 228-0100

Restaurant upstairs, pub downstairs.

Beer everywhere.

Number of different beers: varies
according to time of year (Wildwood
brews special seasonal beers), but
usually seven

Biggest sellers: Wild Wheat, Altitude
Amber, and Long Iron Pilsner

Secret Lounge

You don't
have to be
a university
student to
drink like
one. The Blue Banana Lounge
*(MacEwan Student Centre, near the
bookstore)* operates on Fridays from
3 to 6 p.m., September through
April. Cheap drinks, no cover, black
velvet paintings, and a surprisingly
cool range of musical entertainment.
(Blue Banana alumni include Hayden,
Art Bergmann, and Karl Roth.)

The Night Gallery

The Night Gallery Cabaret comes by its late-night underground rock cred honestly. Back in the '80s, the second-floor room served as home for Golden Calgarians singer/ski bum Bruno, a man notorious for nocturnal revelry. (The GK's "Chicken on the Way," by the by, remains both an ode to greasy greatness and a seminal slab of Calgary punk history.) When Bruno moved along, roommate Greg Baekeland took over the apartment, and thus began the long road to Night Gallerydom: first it was the White Elephant booze can, then the White Elephant Performing Arts Society, then the Night Gallery Artist Run Centre, and now the Night Gallery Cabaret. (Of course, the space was home to the Eagles Fraternity Hall in 1905, the Avenue Ballroom in the '50s, a dance studio in the '60s . . . but that's a whole other story.) Now a half-decade into its latest incarnation, the Night Gallery has hosted a veritable who-who's of indie rock (ranging from local superstars like National Dust and Earthquake Pills to international luminaries like Superchunk), performance-art weirdness (Crispin Glover, Lydia Lunch), and DJs – all the while maintaining its late-night apartment party vibe thanks to a magnificently whacked hodge-podge of pop-culture detritus. (Dig those JFK tapestries.) As for the actual bar itself, it's a teller-wicket rescued from a renovated NE Calgary bank. Traces of patented Royal Bank blue can still be seen on parts of the counter-top.

Glow Bowling

It's ingenious, really: good ol' fashioned bowling, but with glow-in-the-dark balls and pins. The following lanes offer glow-bowling on a regular basis:

Alberta Bowlerama

The Deerfoot Mall location (275-1260) has glow action on Saturdays from 6 p.m. 'til midnight. Over at Franklin Mall (569-2695), it's the same deal from 9 p.m. 'til a staggering 3 a.m.

Chinook Bowladrome

Chinook Centre (basement), 252-5747
Every Saturday from 7 'til to 11 p.m., unless there's a previously-scheduled non-glow tournament.

Clayburn Bowl

1820-52nd St. SE, 248-4664
Every other Saturday, beginning at 6 p.m. Best to phone ahead, just in case.

Frank Sisson's Silver Dollar Bowl

1010-42nd Ave. SE, 287-1183
Frank's Vegas-esque entertainment empire ("Enjoy a drink while you're bowling") is worth checking out on any night, but Fridays (11 p.m. 'til 1 a.m.) is when he breaks out the phosphorescence.

Paradise Lanes and Oasis Lounge

3411-17th Ave. SE, 272-4570
Every Saturday, 9 p.m. 'til midnight.

Toppler Bowl

7640 Fairmount Dr. SE, 255-0101
Offering four nights of fun-in-the-dark, Toppler is the undisputed king of glow-bowling: Tuesdays (6 'til 10 p.m.), Fridays (3:30 p.m. 'til midnight), Saturdays (1:30 p.m. 'til midnight), and Sundays (noon 'til 9 p.m.).

MIDNIGHT IN THE GARDEN OF FOOLS AND RAMSAY

Keep a bloodshot eye open for late-night cabarets at Crump Manor. Home to the Green Fools Physical Theatre Society, the "manor" (1046-18th Ave. SE) is in fact a converted Ramsay service garage (previous tenant: a limousine service) which now houses a 60-seat theatre and the troupe's workshop. The Fools are legendary for walking around on stilts while wearing top-heavy, Euro-creepy masks. (Think Hieronymous Bosch on a papier-mâché bender.) In addition to their regular performances and annual April Fool's Day parade, the Green Fools stage occasional midnight cabarets featuring grotesque clowns, suitably wonky musical entertainment, and an open mic. It's the kinda sticky, witching hour affair that attracts hookers and art students alike (both drunk).

Secret Booze-Cans

Yeah, *right*. How do I know you're not a narc? All I'm saying on record is the city's "unofficial" after-hours joints come and go like the wind. Like the one that used to be under a certain [blank] shoppe, which shut down after that New Year's Eve when a drunk snuck into the storeroom and emerged "wearing" a half-dozen expensive [blanks]. Someone always wrecks the fun, huh? Then there's the handful of Chinatown establishments rumoured to serve up "special tea" (beer in tea pots) 'til the wee hours. And of course, who can forget the downtown pizza parlour notorious for its must-be-happy-hour-somewhere-in-the-world approach to time-telling? (Special 5 a.m. bonus: pissed-up hookers loudly slapping each other in the parking lot.) But that's all I have to say about the matter, so you'll just have to keep your ear to the grindstone.

Golden Triangle

The health-conscious Mission/Cliff Bungalow hipster knows that exercise is the key to a long life of happy slacking. Now you, too, can enjoy the cardio benefits of the low-impact "Golden Triangle" workout. After proper stretching, start with mid-morning breakfast at the Western Coffee Shop (*7, 2100-4th St. SW*). Like its smalltown Alberta cousins, the Western serves both Chinese and (wait for it) "Western" cuisine. The friendliest people on Earth run this classic eggs 'n' wonton greasy spoon. They treat regulars like family, right down to letting them fetch their own coffee refills.

Speaking of coffee, the Western's thin, bean-flavoured brew (not a knock, just an observation) necessitates the two-block saunter to The Planet (*2212-4th St. SW*). Not only does The Planet roast its own damn good coffee, but you can smoke your ass off in its cig-friendly environs. (The truly caffeine-starved, or those experiencing unexpected heart-failure, may wish to kick-start things with a $2 "hi-test" a.k.a. double-espresso topped up with dark coffee.) Now is the time to rest up, for the next grueling leg of the Triangle involves crossing not one but *two* busy streets.

If you've properly paced yourself, the Ship & Anchor Pub (*534-17th Ave. SW*) will have started pouring beer for the thirsty masses. Reward your commitment to physical fitness by drinking Guinness until the wee hours. Remember to properly "cool down" by occasionally walking from the patio to the washroom.

Congratulations! You've now conquered the Golden Triangle – although I guess it's technically the "Golden V" unless you return to the Western Coffee Shop the next morning. (Chin up, champ. Nobody said greatness was gonna be easy.)

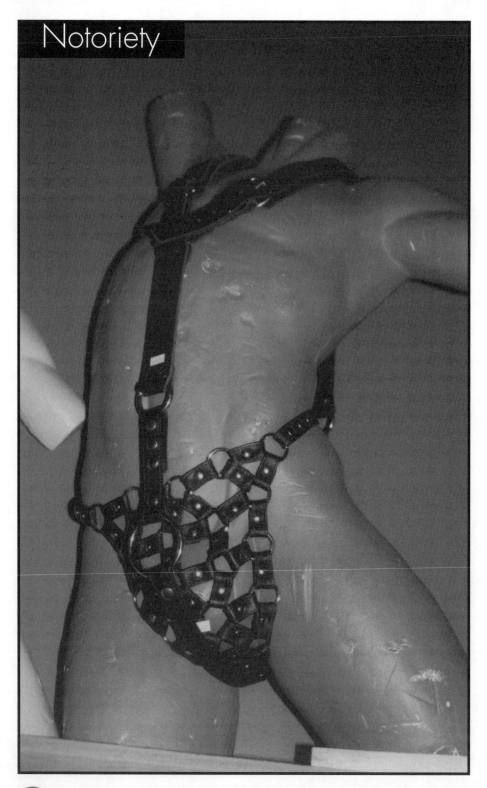

Notoriety

It may *seem* quiet on the surface, but Calgary's Wild West heart is still a-throbbin'. The following pages will tell you where to get your car stolen and how to get elected premier. Warning: this chapter carries a THS (Trigger-Happy Socialite) Rating. The squeamish are advised to avert their eyes and ponder the following philosophical question:
How the heck does David Lee Roth figure into all this?

Godspeed, Scabby Dried Meat

Api-kai-ees (translation: "Scabby Dried Meat") was the swiftest Blackfoot runner, speeding between the Siksika reserve and Calgary like greased lightning. The only thing quicker was word-of-mouth, and he soon earned a reputation as "the fastest runner on the Prairies," kicking serious RCMP butt in various long-distance races. In 1886, a group of Calgary hustlers recruited Api-kai-ees, renamed him "Deerfoot" (paleface marketing at its finest), and entered him in the pro-running circuit. Deerfoot won a lot of races, and his syndicate pals won a lot of money.

That year, *The New York Sporting News* turned out to cover a three-man race between a British running champ, a runner from Ottawa, and Deerfoot. Not surprisingly, Deerfoot was first to cross the finish line – problem was, his backers wagered *against* him, meaning he wasn't supposed to win. A bitter Deerfoot broke with the syndicate and briefly raced as an independent until he was (rather suspiciously, some say) charged with stealing blankets. The accused Deerfoot did what he did best: he ran. After an 18-month manhunt, he turned himself in. The rest of his short life was spent in and out of jail, and he eventually died of tuberculosis while in custody. Deerfoot was buried in an unmarked grave. Years later he was given the white man's highest honour: his name now graces both a mall and a freeway.

Photo: Glenbow Archives NA 18866

When Premier Ralph Klein opens his yap, the results are more fun than the proverbial barrel o' brain-damaged monkeys. Like the time he desperately defended the government's $500M money pit (a.k.a. Swan Hills) as "a tourist attraction." Forget Disneyland, this year let's pack up the kids and visit Canada's only fully-integrated hazardous waste treatment plant! (Been there, done that, absorbed the PCBs.)

Or the time he claimed homeless people are happy people. "I remember old Bob," Klein told reporters at the opening of Centre 110, a Calgary homeless shelter. "The guy used to come down to the racetrack in his bare feet. Barefoot Bob. I've talked to a lot of these people. For the most part they're happy with their lot." (The Klein dictionary defines "the life of Riley" as "sleeping in Riley Park.")

None of which comes as a surprise to Calgarians. Back when he was mayor, Klein shocked our collective pants off with his infamous "creeps and bums" speech of '82. Ralphie told the Calgary Newcomers' Club that the city was being overrun with undesirables ("creeps," "bums") from Eastern Canada. Admitting to being "a bit of a redneck," he proposed "cowboy techniques" to solve the problem, "even if we have to put them all in jail, on top of one another."

But verbal dysentery isn't exclusive to King Ralph's public reign. Klein's twin obsessions (talkin' crap and Eastern Canada) can be traced to his days as a CFCN TV reporter. In '79, the station sent him to Toronto where he conducted man-on-the-street interviews to determine, once and for all, if East hates West. The results were peculiar (a man mysteriously namedropped the Riel Rebellion, a woman praised Vancouver) but in unanimous favour of East-West friendship. Then Ralph chimed in with his own unrelated two-bits. "The key that Toronto is said to have to Canada's political future must of course be used to unlock the minds of her people," he concluded while simultaneously mangling metaphors and mugging in front of the CN Tower, "for they will make the choice and that choice won't stem from attitudes toward Quebec or the West." Uh yeah, what he said.

"X" Marks the Oddball

Michael Moriarty isn't the first visionary to think he can waltz into town and become the big boss. Here's a selective list of notable mayoral also-rans from years gone by:

Jimmy "The Con" Carleton

Photo: Courtesy of the Calgary Sun

(1989): Even in an election boasting a record nineteen candidates, this 75-year-old ex-jailbird stood out in a sea of weird. With 485 fraud convictions under his belt, The Con figured he was well-trained for the political life. He capitalized on the post-Olympic pin craze by selling pins emblazoned with "686" — his very first big house ID number, assigned during a 1947 spell in the Kingston Penitentiary.

Rick "The Dinger" Bell (1998): *The Calgary Sun* columnist and self-styled Bukowskian everyguy racked up 20,916 votes by driving around town in a donated '75 Lincoln Town Car decorated with steer horns. Very impressive, very frightening.

Doug Service (1992, 1995, 1998): A repeat offender, the Bible-thumping electrician "mathematically" calculated that the third time was the charm. It wasn't.

Ron Wise (1998): The so-called "wise choice" wanted to build a "Eurasian land bridge" spanning the Bering Strait. He also believed VLTs to be a front for laundering drug money. Cha-ching.

Floyd Allen (1986, 1989, 1995, 1998): He lives in a trailer surrounded by scrap metal and junked cars. Turn-ons include: being arrested for devouring luncheon meat in supermarkets. Turn-offs: victimization at the hands of a global media conspiracy.

J.R. Foley (1986): It was a malfunction at the junction when the most hated man in Stampede Wrestling threw his hard-hat into the political arena.

George Boychuk (1995): Under the rallying cry of "Free all the cats!" the cabbie-cum-candidate opposed feline-restrictive bylaws. Why? He doesn't like mice.

Chris Teed (1983): Citizen Teed's plan to brighten up city eyesores included painting a mural on the side of the Calgary Tower.

(For)Get Shorty

In 1910, Mr. James Short unsuccessfully petitioned City Council to nix the construction of Chinatown. Short, a lawyer and high school principal, protested that Chinese folks "have not the first idea of cleanliness or sanitation." In 1991, a bunch of big-bucked corporations created the James Short Park, "a tranquil mid-town oasis" with $3/hr. underground parking. Where is this urban paradise, you ask? Smack dab in Chinatown.

No Starch in My Riot Gear, Please

In 1892, a Chinese Calgarian contracted small pox while returning from a visit to the old country. Even though a speedy quarantine prevented a mass outbreak (there were a handful of fatalities all the same), a drunken cricket mob decided to exact revenge against the "yellow menace." Riled up by booze/blistering summer heat/unemployment, 200 angry people took it upon themselves to destroy several laundries and terrorize their Chinese owners. The incident's obvious racist undertones were a civic embarrassment, and the victims were eventually compensated for their losses.

On the Lam (But He Ain't No Sheep)

Fleeing the long arm of the U.S. law, infamous bandito Harry Longabaugh slipped into Alberta during the early 1890s. After a perfectly legal stint breaking horses at the Bar U Ranch in High River (the RCMP once accused him of cruelty to animals, later dropping the charges), he landed in Calgary. Teaming with the notoriously shifty Frank Hamilton, Longabaugh bought an interest in the Grand Central Hotel saloon (*124-9th Ave. SE, long since demolished*). He lived the life of a semi-respectable barkeep until a fateful day in 1893 when the greedy Hamilton withheld his cut of the profits. Utilizing what is today called "negotiation technique," Longabaugh whipped out a pistol, took all the money, and fled to Saskatchewan. Historians are divided as to his final fate. Some say the man also known as the Sundance Kid was gunned down in Bolivia, others claim he now runs a successful indie film festival in Utah.

The Not-So-Great Escape

It doesn't seem like such a bright idea in hindsight, but Calgary's first jail cell was a log cabin. The prison didn't sit empty for very long. The two-man construction crew (lawyers, no less) were so impressed with their handiwork that they overdid it in the celebration department, if you know what I mean, and duly became the jail's first occupants. Ah, but the irony doesn't end there. Intimately familiar with the structure's design flaws, the lawyers took advantage of their insider knowledge and – yep, you guessed it – busted outta the place.

John Jasienczyk (1980, 1983): Drawing on his talk-a-lot experience as an auctioneer, J.J. employed elaborate *Battlestar Galactica* metaphors (really!) to describe the media's vested interest in a puppet mayor. Or something like that.

John Mason (1974, 1977, 1980): Although he claimed to be "the chief kook" during his '74 debut, this parable-spouting driving instructor later changed his tune. The newly-sane Mason asked for voter support only if God ordered them to do so. Apparently He didn't.

Jack Locke (1989, 1992): The gimmick-lovin' baker distributed condoms as a metaphor for the "safety" Calgary would enjoy under an unlimited police budget. Also wore rubber Spock ears.

During his heyday, Tommy Common was Canada's country sweetheart. He sent hearts a-flutter and pulled in thousands of fan letters with his TV appearances on CBC mainstays *Singalong Jubilee*, *The Don Messer Show*, and of course *Country Hoedown*. Like a cowboy Pat Boone, Tommy Common was squeaky-clean, handsome, and sang like a bird.

The Toronto-boy-made-good enjoyed the success. He threw big parties, he drove big cars, and he even opened a chain of "Tommy Common's Teen Town" record stores. But things soured with the cancellation of *Country Hoedown* in '65. Canada's *other* fave Tommy, fellow *Hoedowner* Tommy Hunter, received his own TV show, but Common was cut loose. (Insider gossip claims it's because he was too short.)

After kicking around the showbiz shadows for a boozy decade, Common moved to Calgary with his girlfriend Gail Taylor. An unhappy stint selling real estate spurred him to try politics. In 1979, Common landed a short-lived gig as senior aide to Liberal Senator Bud Olson. Then newly-elected Liberal bossman John Turner cut Olson from his cabinet, leaving Common to once again twist in the wind.

1984 saw Common make an unsuccessful bid for the Liberal nomination in the Bow River riding, after which he was appointed coordinator of Calgary's new anti-vandalism campaign. Clearly shaky on the term "anti-vandalism," Common proceed to drive a car into his girlfriend's backyard and smash her kitchen window with a pitchfork. For an encore, he threatened to torch her St. Bernard and "scatter the ashes around the house."

Two months later, Common spent the morning of August 14, 1985 indulging his two favourite pastimes: drinking a half-bottle of rye and stalking Gail Taylor. Somewhere along the way he selected a Luger from a friend's gun collection. Shortly before noon, he confronted her at gunpoint in front of her Acadia home. As a terrified Taylor turned to flee, Tommy Common fatally shot himself in the head.

Laury Betts (1995): His campaign promises included securing the 2005 Olympics — quite the feat, since there aren't any games scheduled for that particular year.

Terrill Petersen (1992): An ounce of prevention equals a pound of cure, so Petersen proposed reducing "back and joint problems in the population" by recycling tires into soft rubber sidewalks.

Ralph Klein (1980, 1983, 1986): 'Nuff said.

It was perhaps the weirdest paternity suit in legal history: two men squabbling over who sired a race of alien teddy bears. Driving through L.A. in the early '80s, Calgary screenwriter/stuntman/entrepreneur Dean Preston spotted an EWOKS vanity license plate. The incident triggered an apparently dormant memory. Egad, thought Preston, I invented the Ewoks. (Why someone would claim ownership of the saccharine, universally-despised beasts – as opposed to something cool, like Darth Vader – is a bit of a head-scratcher, but that's his story all the same.)

Preston claims he sent an unproduced 1978 script – titled, if you can believe it, *Space Pets* – to George Lucas, who blatantly stole the story's Ewok characters and used them in *Return of the Jedi* (1983). Cowboy Dean, as he was known, filed a $100 million copyright infringement lawsuit in 1985. Five years later, his case surfaced in the Federal Court of Canada. George Lucas flew to Calgary, where he testified he'd never before read *Space Pets,* and any similarities between his and Preston's space bears were "gross" at best. Lucas argued his ownership by delineating the etymology of "Ewok," explaining he reversed the syllables in "Wookie" and then rhymed it with "Miwok." (Lucas is quite familiar with the Miwok tribe; he built his California ranch on their hunting grounds. And some of his best friends are Wookies.) Less convincingly, Preston claimed he invented the word by taking "he walks" and losing the "h."

The "h" wasn't the only thing Dean Preston lost. After two weeks of legal squabbling, the judge ruled that Lucas did no wrong. Preston was ordered to pay the legal costs incurred by Lucas and 20th Century Fox.

Undaunted by his loss, Preston set to work on another space script, this one about a cute alien who visits Earth. The working title is *E.T.* (Joke!)

Take a Bite Outta Crime

(OR AT LEAST LICK IT A LITTLE)

Let's face it: Calgary's pretty tame. Yeah, the Geeky Bandit's 1998 small-haul crime spree made frontpage news, but that was more due to his nerdy good looks and completely whacked choice of targets: seven flower shops, seven coffee/bagel shops, three clothing/fabric stores, three pastry/chocolate shops, two used bookstores, two pet shops, and one specialty cooking shop. (Go for the gold, Geeky.)

That said, the city has its share of bad behavin'. The following theft stats are compiled from the Calgary Police Service website, and refer to a twelve-month period ending in March '99. (As for the absence of murder stats, the front-page of the *Sun* will hafta satisfy your bloodlust.)

Congrats to all our winners, and please save your applause until the end.

Home Burglary

The best place for a homestyle B&E is Connaught (District 1), followed closely by Huntington Hills (District 3) and Rundle (District 4). Remember: always keep an eye open for suspicious activities in/around your neighbours' homes – burglars will often cut you a deal if there's a special something you've been coveting.

Commercial Break-In

Invest in some of those fashionable/practical iron bars if you've set up shop in Downtown Centre (District 1). Hillhurst (District 3) and Manchester (District 1) are tied for distant second.

Break & Enter, Other

I'm not entirely sure what the Police Dept. means by this "other" business, but you'd better nail down your otherness if you live in Pineridge (District 4). Ditto for second-place Ramsay (District 1) and close-third Forest Lawn (District 4).

Auto Theft

Both the Downtown Centre and Marlborough (District 4) are bad places for car theft. (Or good places, if you're a car thief.) The big prize, however, goes to...insert drum roll...our friends in District 2, Bowness. Way to go-go-go, Bownesians!

Theft From Vehicle

Bowness may be #1 in stolen cars, but it didn't make the car-prowling Top Three. (Makes sense: there's no point boosting a radio when you can just take the whole damn car.) First-class honours instead go to Downtown Centre, followed by Victoria Park and Chinatown. All of this category's winners are proud members of District 1.

The Dicks Will Go On

To the untrained eye, this may seem like a shameless attempt to namedrop *Leonardo DiCaprio* – thereby cashing in on the lucrative teenage girl book-buying market – but there really *is* a Calgary-*Titanic* connection. Honest. Back in the day, local real estate tycoon Albert Dick took his teenage bride Vera on a honeymoon cruise thru the Mediterranean, where they collected exotic decorations for their under-construction Mount Royal home (*the appropriately-named Dick House, 2211-7th Street SW*). Eager to start their new life at home, the newlyweds booked passage on that modern miracle, the *RMS Titanic*. Everyone knows what happened next: heavy boat, lots of people, king of the world, iceberg, etc. Vera refused to leave Albert's side and it looked like game-over for the Dicks, but they were piled into a lifeboat at the last minute and lived happily ever after. Or did they? Male *Titanic* survivors were often regarded as yellow-bellies who survived at the expense of a woman or child. Legend has it that Albert Dick was plagued with a cowardly rep throughout his life, and left instructions that he be buried so as to face away from the city which had turned its back on him. (Judge for yourself: hang a left inside the Union Cemetery's Spiller Road entrance, then another left just before the office. Keep trucking uphill. The Dicks are buried on the northern tip of section L. Their headstone is almost completely hidden under a hedge.) Then there was the time the real estate market soured and the Dicks lost their fortune, but that's another story. Roll credits, cue Céline Dion.

Nothing to See Here, Folks

The biggest thing to hit Calgary in 1913 (pugilistically speaking) was the fight between Arthur Pelkey and Luther McCarthy. A special arena was even built in Manchester to accommodate the bloodthirsty masses. McCarthy sustained a neck injury before the fight, but the show went on as scheduled. Early in the first round, Pelkey knocked his opponent to the canvas with a surprisingly light blow to the head. Minutes later, McCarthy was pronounced dead.

White Hat, White Heat

With binary symbolism straight out of a John Wayne flick, Calgary uses a white cowboy hat to welcome distinguished visitors. The practice flourished throughout the 1950s, until City Council voted to drastically reduce the number of White Hat presentations. (Insert sound of pennies being pinched.) The Calgary Convention and Visitors Bureau eventually took over the tradition.

Although any ol' schlub can receive a White Hat (all you gotta do is call the CCVB Warehouse at 266-6340 and cough up the $20-$70 per chapeau, depending whether you want straw or felt), the city still uses the ceremony to honour select individuals.

It's fun to look at who does/doesn't receive the City Hall thumbs-up. Chinese bigwigs Zhu Rongji (Prime Minister) and Jian Zemin (President) recently received the royal White Hat treatment when they rolled into Calgary on separate visits. (Ronghi gave "discount travel" a new meaning when he offered to fly naysayers to Tibet so they could get a firsthand taste of the joy that is militarized occupation. Zemin is best known for his iron-fisted role in the '89 Tiananmen Square massacre – tanks for the memories, Big J!) On a completely unrelated note (winkety-wink), China is poised to become a major player in Cowtown's economy. Local company Asia Pacific Concrete Inc., for example, is set to sink $4.25M into a ready-mix concrete plant located in Taiyuan, China. (Fun fact: Kit Chan, the mayor's wife, sits on the Asia Pacific Concrete board of directors.)

On the flipside, City Hall didn't give White Hats to either Wei Jingsheng (three-time Nobel prize nominee and dissident jailbird) or Wang Dan (the main student leader at Tiananmen, also an ex-jailbird). Jingsheng was particularly miffed; never one to let a hockey rivalry drop, the city of Edmonton presented him with a *black* hat.

The question remains: why did Wei Jingsheng and Wang Dan go hatless? To solve this mystery, we shall deconstruct the winning style of Mr. David Lee Roth, a proud White Hat recipient during his early '80s heyday with goodtime rockers Van Halen.

1. David Lee Roth is a world-famous entertainer who sold millions of records. Jingsheng and Dan spent thousands of hours in jail.

2. David Lee Roth once had sex with two strippers in a bed full of money. Jingsheng and Dan slept in beds full of bugs.

Special Bonus: Vandalism!

It was a Grade A sob story: Tim Cuell's Acadia house was extensively trashed days after Christmas '98. Or was it? Further inspection revealed carefully "destroyed" yet functional appliances and hilariously generic graffiti. (Why spray-paint squiggly lines when there's so many delightful 4-letter words?) It began to look like Cuell was his own worst vandal (read: insurance fraud) and charges were laid.

Acadia may be safe from vandals, but Downtown Centre isn't. In fact, it's the city's #1 vandalism hot-spot. (Vandalism aesthetes take note: you can still see vintage 1980s "Statue of Liberty with handgun" spray-paint stenciling in certain alleys between 8th & 9th Aves.) Distant second place goes to Victoria Park. And the third place ribbon goes to our old pal Bowness.

P.S. The astute reader may be thinking, "Gee whizzikers, Districts 5 & 6 must be the safest place in the city. I'm moving!" Don't pack those bags just yet. There is indeed a District 6, but there's *no* District 5. I repeat: District 5 *does not exist*. (It's a cop thing, don't ask.)

NUN'S GARDEN

Ah, science squelches magic once again. For years, local folklore had it that nuns buried stillborn babies in a small garden at the north end of the Holy Cross Hospital. It was a tiny gesture to give some small comfort to grieving mothers — a tiny gesture that didn't sound so poetic after the hospital's closure. (I guess potential renters weren't so keen on the pitter-patter of ghostly feet.) Enter the ground-penetrating radar. After an extensive sweep of the area, the Calgary Regional Health Authority announced that nobody was ever buried in the "Nun's Garden." Firm believers still cling to the legend, however, even going as far as to suggest the *real* cemetery is underneath the adjacent parking lot. The Nun's Garden isn't much to look at today (the Virgin Mary grotto and ivy-covered fence have been replaced by a storage shed and heaps of plywood), but you can check out the vibe for yourself. Turn left onto Holy Cross Lane from 2nd St. SW; that's the garden on the right, just before the street curves south.

3. David Lee Roth scored a "personal best" record by bedding five women at the same time, including a pair of sisters. Jingsheng and Dan have accomplished nothing with their lives, except for laze about in jail.
4. David Lee Roth employs two midget security guards, and he dresses 'em in kooky matching outfits. All you can say about Jingsheng and Dan is they're not in jail anymore, and that's pretty faint praise if you ask me.

Conclusion: Chinese freedom-fighters should stop whining and start wearing tighter pants.

Blues Babylon

The sun may be shining and the birds may be chirping, but it's permanent midnight inside the King Eddy (*438-9th Ave. SE*). The hotel's $23/night rooms may be wholly unexceptional, but the bar's stage has hosted almost every blues legend you can think of: Buddy Guy, Junior Wells, Pinetop Perkins, Robert Jr. Lockwood, Koko Taylor, Otis Rush…. True to form, the Eddy has seen just as much action offstage, with wizened bluesmen exorcising/medicating their personal hellhounds any which way they can. The debauchery is legendary, and many stories end with punchlines like "…only to find the bass player schlepping his girlfriend upstairs" or "…passed out in the hallway, wearing only a turban." Respectful of the music, nobody in the club's inner circle will go on record with the sordid details. (The closest you'll get is the time Crowbar were barbecuing steaks on the fire escape and set off all the fire alarms.) Buy an Eddy regular a couple of beers, however, and you just might learn somethin'.

Photo: Courtesy of the Calgary Sun

Here's a question for Martha Stewart: what do you serve at the year's hottest attempted murder? Handgun-shaped paté? Bullet shells stuffed with crab? Hot lead and cold beer?

On January 21, 1995, socialite Dorothy Joudrie pumped six rounds into her estranged husband. Then, as he lay crumpled on the garage floor of her Bearspaw condo, she calmly called 911. Earl Joudrie survived, and Calgary got its very own O.J.-styled media circus.

Dorothy and Earl Joudrie were married for 30 years, and separated for five at the time of the shooting. Earl Joudrie was the sixtysomething chairman of Gulf Canada Resources, Algoma Steel, and Canadian Tire. People called him "The Plumber" because of his uncanny ability to sweep in and save corporations from going down the toilet. People called Dorothy "The Hostess With The Mostest" because she threw a damn good party. The Plumber wanted a divorce. The Hostess, apparently, had other ideas.

According to various testimonies given during the three-week long trial, The Plumber was an abusive jerk (he allegedly tried to cure his wife's fear of heights by speeding along precarious mountain roads – on their honeymoon) and The Hostess was a boozehound. The Hostess claimed she "accidentally" smuggled her .25 calibre Beretta across the border, forgetting it under the seat of her red Jaguar when she motored home from Arizona – but remembering to secure it in a fanny-pack (safety first!) when she later sold the car. The defense team argued Dorothy shot Earl while in a robotic, dissociative state. The prosecution countered these

BLACK FRIDAY

Phillipe Gagnon didn't build models, but he bought a lot of airplane glue. The local grocery store soon grew tired of feeding his fume habit and cut him off. On December 20, 1974, an irritated Gagnon threatened the owner, who in turn called the cops. When two police officers later approached the converted garage Gagnon called home, the glue-sniffer responded with gunfire. Backup was called, and Officer Boyd Davidson was killed in the ensuing battle. (The fatal bullet splintered on impact and injured six other policemen.) The Ramsay

claims of automatism by citing Dorothy's rather lucid 911 calls. Even after a vigorous shooting, The Hostess gave good directions. (Hey, what's the point of throwing a party if your guests can't find the place?)

On May 9, 1996, Dot was found "not criminally responsible" due to zombism. She was sent to an Edmonton mental hospital for appraisal, during which time she had her nose busted by a fellow patient. Meanwhile, The Plumber married her second cousin.

For all you sicko rubberneckers wishing to take a peek at the $350,000 scene of the crime, why not take the handy directional advice of Mrs. Roboto herself, as supplied to a 911 operator: "It's 143 Country Club Lane. You come up Crowchild to Bearspaw Road ... make a right on Hamilton Drive and make a right into Bearspaw Country Club Estates....

"I'll open the garage door."

neighbourhood was evacuated, streets were sealed off, and a crowd of police and reporters formed around the garage. Holed up in a primitive cellar, Gagnon survived a tear-gas assault because his nostrils were so gummed up with airplane glue. Periodic gunfire punctuated the hours-long standoff. The police finally borrowed a tank from the Canadian Forces Base and leveled the garage. Running from his hideout with guns a-blazing, Gagnon was killed in a hail of bullets. With one officer dead and eight injured, the day lives on in police history as "Black Friday."

Purty Woman

What's a world-class city without a famous hooker? Los Angeles has Heidi Fleiss. New York has Sydney Biddle Barrows. And Calgary has Pearl Miller. By all accounts a squat woman partial to (mercifully) over-rouging her homely mug, Pearl left interior B.C. in the 1920s to set up shop on Calgary's 9th Avenue. The son of a prominent local lawyer was so taken with Pearl (as a friend, naturally) that he set her up in a fancy house on Macleod Trail, just outside what was then the city limits. Pearl's place catered to a wealthy oil clientele who would stop in for a quick "game of bridge" when travelling to/from the fields. Pearl was good to the itchy wildcats and they were in turn good to Pearl – so good, in fact, that she moved her operation to posh Mount Royal in 1935. Pearl retired in 1950 and died in 1957. She got religion in her twilight years and spent much of her time trying to reform the working girls down on the 9th Avenue stroll.

Pearl's reputation was the stuff of legend and/or baloney. One unsubstantiated story concerned a group of WWII Canadian soldiers. When neighbouring American GIs raised a "Remember Pearl Harbor!" banner, the Canadians responded with their own declaration: "To hell with Pearl Harbor! Remember Pearl Miller!" You too can remember Pearl Miller by eyeballing her former Mount Royal digs at 1813-9th St. SW.

Instead of a Parade, Can I Just Have the Cash?

Pee Wee Smith clinched his place as a Stampeder fan fave when he completed an eleventh-hour 67-yard touchdown reception, handily winning the 1991 Western Final. The following year, Smith and the Stamps stomped the Blue Bombers to claim the Grey Cup. Six years later, off the gridiron thanks to a buggered knee, Smith hocked his Grey Cup ring at the Pawnshop Superstore (3520-17th Ave. SE). A Calgary Sun newshound uncovered the story and an embarrassed Smith retrieved the ring. Not a moment too soon, either: Smith's buyback period had lapsed and the pawnshop was entertaining offers from interested collectors. The alleged pawn price – for those of you looking to unload an Oscar statuette or Most Improved Attendance ribbon – was $8,000.

She's Got Legs and Knows How to Use 'Em

As a rule of thumb, contemporary unkempt garbage-pickers are "gross," while historical unkempt garbage-pickers are "colourful." Thanks to the kindness of time, turn-of-the-century eccentric Caroline "Mother" Fulham falls into the latter category. The foul-mouthed Fulham patrolled the alleys of downtown Calgary, collecting restaurant leftovers in her trash-wagon. The refuse was then fed to the pigs she kept in her 6th Ave. house, much to the pleasure of downwind neighbours. (She also had a cow, but it was killed by a passing train. Fulham sued CP Rail because the innocent beast was unable to read the "No Trespassing" sign.) As legend has it, Mother Fulham once required medical attention for a badly injured leg. The attending physician was so disgusted by her hygiene (or lack thereof) that he wagered there wasn't a filthier limb in Calgary. You can probably guess the punchline: not one to lose a $5 bet, Ma Fulham proudly showed him her other leg.

Barenaked Ladies (Men, Too)

New York's infamous sex districts are on the outs thanks to rigorous new anti-smut regulations (i.e., nothing XXX within view of a school, church, park, hot-dog cart, pigeon, etc.). So praise the nakedness gods that Calgary still has its share of live flesh. For those of you who've read every book in the library and still have idle hours to fill until the big Scrabble championship, here's a selective tour of Skin City.

TIGHT CLOTHES

Hooters
4608 Macleod Trail SW
Hooters is a restaurant, a fact that surprises much of its slack-jawed, drool-stained clientele. What a formula: tiny white T-shirts, orange short-shorts, and crummy food. Daisy Duke would be proud.

By 1997, Marilyn Manson was a household name, his warmed-over Alice Cooper aesthetic (and Ziggy Stardust pretensions) having long endured him to disaffected teens the world over. Heck, he'd even earned his own Ozzy-styled urban legends: Manson *kills* audience members! Manson hands out *drugs* at his concerts! Manson *kills* his fans, *resurrects* them, and then gets the *zombie teens* hooked on *drugs!* (Naturally, the rumours were complete bunk, if only because they violate the #1 rule of rock marketing: dead kids don't buy T-shirts.)

'Tis no surprise that tickets sales were brisk for Marilyn Manson's July 25, 1997 concert in the Max Bell Centre, no doubt music to owner Larry Ryckman's cash register. But, upon opening a $152,000 property tax bill, Ryckman realized that Marilyn Manson was in fact the devil. Ryckman confirmed this horrible truth with his mom and knew something must be done. Wearing his freshly-minted morality on his sleeve, he canceled the upcoming concert and recruited the aid of then-alderman (and future mayoral candidate/loser) Ray Clark. Together, the dynamic duo waged war against the so-called Antichrist Superstar, calling the shock-rocker's concert "not suitable for family entertainment."

The show did not go on. Many cities moaned about Marilyn, but Calgary did something about it, dagnammit!

The international spotlight shone brightly on the Bible Beltbuckle, earning Calgary the kind of press usually reserved for Salt Lake City.

Like a heroic Puritan straight out of a Hawthorne story (albeit a heroic Puritan once found guilty of stock manipulation and subsequently banned from the security-trading biz), Larry Ryckman had rid his fair city of Satan. The forces of evil at bay, Ryckman turned his attention to those pesky city taxes. Surely his efforts would be "rewarded," no? Sadly, it would seem morality is its own reward: the city seized Ryckman's arena and Universal Concerts successfully sued him for breach of contract (to the tune of $43,756). An exhausted Ryckman later moved to Arizona. Guess the old saying is true: the only sure things in life are death-rock and taxes.

Cowboy's Dance Hall

826-5th St. SW

The bar-equivalent of Hooters. Female employees are supposedly eligible for a gratis boob job after working a year. (There's also a lopsided, less reliable rumour making the rounds: six months for the left breast, six months for the right.) Cowboy's features an eclectic, anything-that's-remotely-popular booking policy. The incurably curious are advised to wait until Run DMC or Blue Öyster Cult are playing, just in case oglin' ain't enough.

Mummy Dearest

Thomas Hall held many jobs (chicken farmer, stock trader, teamster), but the thing he apparently did best was criticize. By 1929, Hall had driven off two wives and his oldest son, leaving him alone with his fifteen-year-old boy. The lucky youngster, John, was now the sole target for Daddy's abuse – until Daddy abruptly disappeared. Hall's family continued on with their lives, not terribly upset by their loss. With Thomas Hall MIA, the family homestead (1805-20th Ave. NW) was turned over to the bank and eventually sold to the Pearce family in 1948. But something about the house just didn't feel right. After experiencing bad vibes in the back bedroom, the Pearces ripped up the floorboards and discovered – surprise! – the well-mummified body of Thomas Hall. (Cause of death: two big holes in his skull.) An investigation followed, but charges were never laid.

Bigamist Wigs Out

In 1911, transplanted Alabama businessman John C. Davis married local gal Minnie Black. Davis proved a jealous/abusive hubby and hired an amateur detective named Mildred Dixon to tail his wife. After seeing bite marks on Minnie's arms, Mildred realized the hubby's true nature and shifted her loyalties. Fearing for her safety, Minnie moved into Mildred's 17th Ave. apartment. Davis quickly sniffed 'em out. Waving their marriage certificate in one hand and a pistol in the other, he burst into the second-floor room; Davis fatally shot the two women before turning the gun on himself. Weeks later, police discovered "John C. Davis" was really Spencer Holder, a bigamist with a wife and kids back in Alabama. Nailbiting historians take note: the scene of the crime is now home to The Magic Room (602-17th Ave. SW), a great place to buy a wig or get a manicure.

176

Year-Round Birthday Suits

The back room at the King Eddy Hotel isn't your typical refuge for randy oil tycoons. Rumoured to employ one-legged dancers and the like, the Eddy is a feelgood story of triumph-over-adversity (not to mention really good balance). More "traditional" peeler clubs include:

The Original French Maid
302-3rd Ave. SW

The French Maid's Speakeasy Adult Sports Pub
6307 Centre St. S

Misty's Exotic Show Lounge
3440 Bow Trail SW

Sirens Exotic Entertainment
1235-73rd Ave. SE

The Shoppe
4127-6th St. NE

Finally, for those craving an equal opportunity eyeful, Dooie Stevens Nightclub & Tavern *(3440 Bow Trail SW)* offers nekkid gentlemen on Thursdays and Saturdays. Go nuts.

The Telus Convention Centre expansion *(north side of Stephen Ave. Walk, between 1st St. SE and Centre St.)* has been dogged by controversy every step of its awkward birth. First there was the pesky inconvenience of all those old buildings opposite the original Convention Centre: knock 'em down or keep 'em up? The resulting compromise (incorporate the historical façades into the new building) is better than nothing, but the block just isn't the same without the Calgary Shoe Hospital's super-cool sign. (Unlike the General or Holy Cross, however, the Shoe Hospital soldiers on at a nearby new location.) The Crown Building wasn't so lucky: restaurateur Lawrence Romanosky wanted to move the building across the street next to his Auburn Saloon (at his expense, no less), but more demolition-minded heads prevailed. And then there was the bylaw snafu in which the city broke its own rules by pushing thru construction without proper title registration. (A 66-foot strip of land fell through the cracks. Sixty-six feet?!? Now that's a big crack.)

Tongues are a-wag with gossip: is the expansion being sloppily fast-tracked in order to cash in on the 2000 World Petroleum Congress – so sloppy, in fact, that the facility is destined for untimely obsolescence? Is the new convention centre a shortsighted grab for quick cash? Maybe, maybe not. But one thing's for sure: it ain't cheap. At time of writing, city hall approved a third cost overrun, bringing the project to $65M.

index

index

179

index

index

index

index

index

index

index

index

JAMES MARTIN has lived in Calgary since 1979, and is a graduate of Silver Springs Elementary School. He is the ex-editor (fired) of the semi-defunct rock/roll monthly *VOX,* and now writes the weekly "Mr. Smutty" column for *FFWD* magazine. Martin co-wrote the feature film *Way Downtown* (with writer/director Gary Burns), and is a regular contributor to *Where Calgary.* He has also written for *Sassy,* but only once.